Beyond the PPL

Beyond the PPL

Putting the fun and skill into flying

Nigel Everett

Airplan Flight Equipment Ltd

ISBN 1 874783 29 2

Published by

Airplan Flight Equipment Ltd

1a Ringway Trading Estate, Shadowmoss Road, Manchester M22 5LH

Tel: 0161 499 0023   Fax: 0161 499 0298

www.afeonline.com

Acknowledgements

Many people have helped me with this book and I thank them all. In particular I sincerely thank Michael Goodwin, who prepared most of the diagrams and took part in many of the photographic sorties. I thank Captain Eric Thurston, whose advice on engine handling on take-off appears herein; and Dr Jan Hedergård for his concept of the Dinghy Captain and his/her duties which I have borrowed.

I also thank all those people who kindly loaned photographs or modelled themselves, their premises or their aircraft. These include the Royal Air Force, Airplan Flight Equipment Ltd, Anglo-American Airmotive Ltd, Wycombe Air Park Ltd, Michael Goodwin, Graham Pratt, Nigel Skinner, Richard Webber, South Warwickshire Flying School, air traffic controllers at Exeter Airport, the Aeronautical Information Service, Halfpenny Green Flight Centre Ltd, Dermot and Debbie Richardson, Jan and Bryony Bradford, my wife, Jean, and Exeter Flying Club. My thanks also to countless other pilots, some friends, some writers, some just names on the Internet whose ideas and recommendations I have always found stimulating even where I have entirely disagreed with them.

To Jean

This book is intended to be a guide after gaining a PPL. It is **NOT** a definitive interpretation of any law, regulation, procedure or information. In the UK the main 'competent authority' regarding interpretation and applicability of rules, regulations and procedures is the Civil Aviation Authority, to whom such questions should be addressed in the first instance. More so than any other aspect of flying, rules, regulations and procedures change on a regular basis. It is good airmanship and sound aviation practice to regularly up-date and check your knowledge of Communications and Air Law rules, regulations and procedures.

Contents

The Author

Nigel Everett is an aviation writer who has been a regular contributor to flying magazines and is now the editor of Flight Safety, the quarterly magazine of the General Aviation Safety Council, with a circulation of around 15,000.

Starting flying when he was only 17, he was fortunate enough to be taught to fly in the RAF and trained on Piston Provosts and Vampires (FB5s and T11s). Having gained his wings, he concluded an undistinguished military career by crashing a Chipmunk.

Since then he has continued flying as a private pilot for recreation and on business. He is not a flying instructor and looks at private flying from the private pilot's point of view. This means dealing with difficulties caused by flying relatively few hours a year and the ever-present problem of the cost of flying if you have to pay for it out of your own pocket. Above all, private flying has to be fun and it has to be safe.

Previous books by Nigel Everett:

Attitude – A Guide to Advanced Flying Training and Tests (jointly with Hugh John)

Everett's Guide to Flying Training in the UK – 1996

Everett's Guide to Flying Training in the UK – 1997

Introduction

The world is full of qualified aeroplane and microlight private pilots who are unsure of what to do with their expensive and hard-earned qualifications. The world may be full of them, but the skies are empty. Having taken a few admiring friends and relations around the local flying area, the newly fledged private pilot often feels a loss of motivation and wonders whether the rather limited fun being had is really worth the considerable cost. There is a marked sense of anti-climax and a tendency to wander around the sky like a lost dog, often followed by a loss of interest in flying at all. The aeroplane flying school will quite probably suggest taking a Night Rating or an IMC Rating. But to someone who has laboured long and hard to be allowed to fly unsupervised by an instructor, the attractions of yet more dual instruction, more ground school and more flying tests are distinctly limited.

The Private Pilot's Licence (PPL) itself is seen more or less as the ultimate goal of the private student pilot. However, a pilot who has gained the PPL as the first step towards obtaining a commercial pilot's licence will have several 'next steps' in the long ladder to be climbed. Equally, a military pilot who reaches PPL standard will continue with flying training for a good while yet. Only at about 250 hours – compared with the 60 hours or so of the PPL – does he or she proceed to operational training.

What all this means is that the Private Pilot's Licence should be seen as no more than a licence to go out and learn some more. In that sense it is the equivalent of the driving licence, and anyone who holds one of these for a year or so is very well aware that much is now known about driving that was not known when the test was passed. If the PPL resembles the driving licence in that respect, it also offers the great advantage that you are not required to have another driver (or an instructor) sitting alongside you as you extend your knowledge and experience.

An RAF pilot receives his wings

Having passed your driving test, you could quite easily find yourself driving solo for six or twelve hours a week. Very few PPLs are going to be flying twelve hours a week, or even twelve hours a month. So their rate of improvement is likely to be a great deal slower than that of the car driver, and consequently their self-confidence is likely to become a rather tender flower. Without it, however, no pilot is likely to get much enjoyment out of flying. The name of the game is therefore to build carefully and progressively on the skills already learned and allow confidence to build as well. The eventual aim is that you should feel confident in your ability to cope with a VFR flight anywhere in western Europe. From this confidence will come increasing enjoyment in every flight.

As we have seen, the student commercial pilot on an approved training course and the student military pilot both continue beyond PPL standard with structured and defined training paths. But the ordinary PPL and the self-improver hoping eventually to gain a professional licence are cast out into the outer darkness. For visual flying (VFR) by day the Civil Aviation Authority (CAA) offers no further goal for the PPL, although there is a yawning gap between the standards of VFR flying of the newly qualified PPL and the experienced and truly competent VFR pilot. There is a curious contrast here between the world of private powered flight (supervised by the CAA) and the world of gliding (supervised by the British Gliding Association) where there is an endless succession of goals from the humble Bronze Badge up to the highly coveted and rarely achieved Diamond. In the world of yachting there are similarly ascending qualifications administered by the Royal Yachting Association. But the CAA apparently sees no need for further goals in VFR flying for the PPL. If such goals were offered, even if their achievement conferred no extra privileges, flying training schools would be setting out their stalls and persuading their customers to train for the "Senior PPL" or whatever.

The typical PPL is not usually very keen on undertaking much dual tuition from an instructor beyond the occasional check ride, and the difference in cost between dual and solo aircraft-hire rates creates a powerful disincentive to electing to take an instructor along. The likely way forward for the PPL will therefore mainly involve solo flying, or perhaps mutual flights shared with another PPL. I have assumed that many of the flights and exercises will be undertaken solo although some will require a demonstration by an instructor at first, leaving the pilot subsequently to improve technique by solo practice.

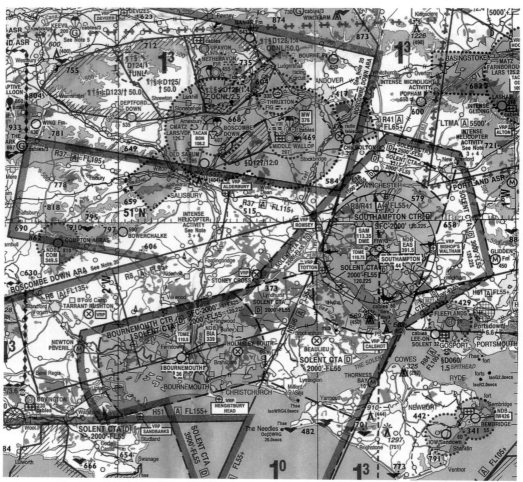

Could you confidently fly across this area?

The book deals with three main areas:

1 Aircraft handling. You advance only a little further than the manoeuvres learned as part of the PPL syllabus, but you greatly improve your accuracy of flying and your appreciation of the effects of airspeed and loading on handling. I remind you that "Loss of control" is a common cause of fatalities in light-aircraft accidents, and work with you in enhancing your appreciation of the common causes of loss of control, how to recognize and avoid them.

2 Navigation. Low-level, cross-country, radio and GPS navigation are all developed and practised.

3 Radio and Clearances. My aim is that by the time you have mastered these further skills, you will be able to fly VFR with confidence in any airspace up to Class D; to boldly enter and leave Control Areas; and to cross national boundaries.

While the book has an obvious appeal to the recently qualified PPL, I believe that even experienced private pilots will find plenty of interesting challenges within these pages. Any pilot who imagines that there is nothing more to be learned about flying is likely to be missing out on yet more challenges to be met and satisfaction to be had.

Safe flying, and be sure to enjoy yourself!

Nigel Everett

WARNING

If you set out to extend your knowledge and expand your experience in flying, as in virtually anything else, you will be venturing into unknown territory. The air is a very unforgiving environment and small mistakes can prove disastrous to the pilot without sufficient skill or experience. As a guide into such dangerous and alien territory, no book is sufficient on its own.

While it is assumed that the exercises in this book will frequently be practiced solo by the PPL reader, you are warned that none of them should be undertaken solo unless first performed under the supervision of a flying instructor, until such time that the latter approves their further practice on a solo basis.

Furthermore, check rides should be undertaken with a flying instructor at intervals to ensure that no bad habits or dangerous practices have been formed during solo practice.

What do you need?

What do you need?

Chapter 1

In addition to your well-deserved PPL, you need:

- An aircraft,
- Personal equipment, and
- Money

To elaborate:

The Aircraft

The aircraft which you used for your training will probably do well enough, certainly as far as handling exercises are concerned. For VFR navigation the same aeroplane may well be suitable, but in my view you do need an aircraft fitted with a transponder – preferably with Mode C altitude reporting or before long, Mode S. Many training aircraft these days have transponders, and I believe that apart from simple local flying in an area where there is no secondary surveillance radar, you should be squawking 7000 (for a VFR flight) with altitude selected if you can. Many inexperienced pilots are dubious about the attractions of a transponder. Basically, they fear being overseen by the Fat Controller from whom, if they are squawking, no secrets will be hidden. It is very important for your future progress to get out of this mind-set and accept radar control for the greater degree of safety which it undoubtedly provides.

Most controllers actually want to help pilots, in spite of rumours to the contrary. If ATC has an accurate and continual readout of your position and height, they are in a better position to assist. If, however, they have no more than doubtful radar blips occasionally confused by conflicting position reports, they get frustrated and sometimes even tetchy. So the more you can do to let the controller know where you are and what you are going to do next, the more relaxed and helpful a service you are likely to get. Where there is secondary radar, any controller is going to feel happy about an aircraft equipped with a transponder – even more so if it has Mode C – and disappointed at an aircraft with no squawk.

A Transponder. The next most useful avionics set on board after your radio. This one has Mode C altitude reporting

There is sometimes something to be said for a four-seater aircraft as opposed to the more usual two-seat trainer where three or four aviators are willing to share practice flights. Even sitting in the back seat, you can learn a lot from observing some other pilot going through an exercise. Choose an aircraft with intercom in the back seats as well as the front.

Make sure that whatever aircraft you use has a really good radio. There are some aircraft around with indifferent radios and these will make life much more difficult for you. There is no need to suffer the confusion, frustration and aggravation of poor radio and intercom communications, since there are plenty of aircraft with good units. So do yourself a favour and make sure that yours is one of them.

A microlight pilot will probably have become an aircraft owner before getting the PPL so that for many the choice will already have been made. If you are thinking of upgrading to a higher performance microlight then be sure to get adequate training on the new machine. It may well be faster and more complicated than what you were used to previously and it is not wise to try to train yourself to cope with

"Even sitting in the back seat you can learn a lot from observing..."

its greater demands. During a self taught training process you are going to be at considerable risk and it is far better to be introduced carefully and methodically to the new microlight's needs by someone already familiar with it. If it flies significantly faster than its predecessor you will find at first that everything seems to happen before you are ready.

Personal Equipment

You will already have most of what you need from your PPL training days. Make sure that you have up-to-date maps and access to the POH/FM for your particular aircraft. It is very helpful to have a photocopy of at least parts of the manual so that you can do weight and balance, take-off/landing distance, fuel consumption and similar calculations at home before a flight. Trying to do these half an hour before take off is a difficult and often fruitless task, especially if you are not in practice with them and not familiar with that particular manual.

A regular supply of aviation magazines will keep you touch with the world of private flying and I also commend the 'General Aviation Safety Sense' leaflets issued (for free!) by the CAA. At the time of writing there were 25 of them although additions on further subjects may be published yet, and updates to existing leaflets are issued from time to time.

Try not to bedeck yourself with a whole range of clever gadgets which will simply take up too much time and attention when their moment comes. You don't *really* need a gadget to tell you the downwind and base-leg heading for a left-hand circuit for runway 21. Just concentrate on identifying the correct runway when you get to a strange airfield and go round the circuit by eye, concentrating on lookout and going round in the prescribed direction.

Never take to the air without pencil and paper. For preference, make that two or more pencils because if you have only one it will assuredly end up on the floor out of reach. The purpose of these essentials is to write down the vital figures from radio calls; the reason you need to do this is (if you have not yet noticed it) that the brain seems to atrophy in the air to about one and a half effective cells. Quite often these become fully employed in some pressing matter such as changing tanks or setting up a new heading, after which you find that you have entirely forgotten the frequency which you so confidently read back two minutes ago. When you "read back" a radio call you really should be *reading* it – which means that you should have written down the essentials before you read them back. Controllers are neither surprised nor annoyed if there is a pause between their call and your readback, because they expect you to be writing as they are speaking and finishing writing after they have finished. So always take pencil and paper, and always write down before you read back.

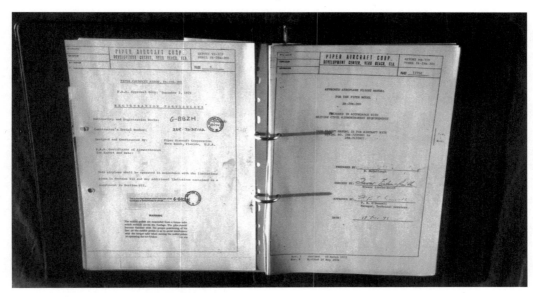

The Pilot's Operating Handbook or Flight Manual

Your knee board with some sort of nav. plot and airfield plans for your destination and alternates are vital ingredients of a successful trip. You will also be taking along a properly marked up map – and lots of pens/pencils

Money

You always hoped that flying would become cheaper when you had got your PPL. You were probably beguiled by the flying school's favourite scenario of you taking up countless friends and relations – perhaps in one of the school's four-seaters – and persuading them all to contribute their due share of the cost of the flight. Most PPLs soon find that the number of their friends and relations willing to contribute to a pilot's flying costs on a regular basis are exceeding small. Indeed, most PPLs find that the only potential cost-sharers to be found on a regular basis are other pilots. At first sight this may seem a little disappointing, in that cost-sharing pilots are no doubt going to want to share the controls as well. So you pay in full for your time at the controls and you receive some free passenger time in addition, but at the cost of having to accommodate the requirements of your partner. Be not cast down! Other pilots are in fact the very best sharers you could find. There is not usually much new to be learned as a pilot from taking your somewhat reluctant neighbour over your respective houses – it's probably something of a milk run for you. Admittedly, I do know of one PPL whose neighbour observed from 1500ft overhead a strange car in the drive and the bedroom curtains drawn in the middle of the afternoon, but nothing significant of an aeronautical nature was learned from that flight.

If, however, you share flights with another pilot you have a chance to form a *crew*; to learn to work together as a team in which you both play a full part. You gain confidence from this and you improve you ability. You are operating as a crew member for the whole of the flight, you are learning all the time and you are sharing the cost.

A further way of reducing the cost of flying can be to become an aircraft owner. Well, yes, I do know that this can also be a way of dramatically increasing the cost of your flying, so do take care not to get carried away by the idea but examine every proposition with due care. Some kind soul might generously offer you the chance of buying his all-singing all-dancing flying machine awash with knobs, bells, whistles and horsepower, and assure you that ownership of this exciting machine will greatly reduce the cost of your flying as well as enhancing its thrill. If so, make your excuses and leave.

The economics of aircraft ownership are both simple and remorseless. There are fixed costs which are incurred even if the aircraft never leaves the ground but merely stands there ready for use. These usually include insurance, hangarage, annual and triennial checks, use of capital and depreciation. For a simple single-engined aircraft these fixed costs amount typically to perhaps £3000 to £7000 per year. If the aircraft flies only 50 hours a year, the fixed costs alone will amount to £60-140 per hour. In addition there will be running costs – fuel, oil, maintenance, landing fees and so on. What this all tends to add up to is that any aircraft needs to be used for at least 250 hours per annum if the fixed costs are to be sufficiently spread to diminish to an acceptable level by most people's standards. It follows that unless you intend to use your aircraft for something more than 250 hours a year, you are not likely to find exclusive ownership an economical form of aircraft operation. Indeed, I have to conclude that almost any private pilot who is an exclusive owner is either flying far more hours a year than do most private pilots or has decided to accept a very high cost per hour as the price of sole ownership.

Sharing an Aircraft

It is hardly surprising, therefore, that the average "aircraft-owning" private pilot turns out to be the proprietor of no more than a share in an aircraft. Aircraft sharing is a well-established practice in the UK, and at the end of the 'For Sale' section of the classified advertisements at the back of any flying magazine – especially *Popular Flying* – you will find groups looking for new members. The number of sharers can extend under CAA rules to 20, but between three and six represents the common range for the number of partners in a group. What each group is looking for is enough partners to spread the cost of the initial share, and the monthly fixed costs widely enough to keep these figures affordable. But on the other hand, they also want to keep the number of members small enough to guarantee good availability for each partner. The common perception of aircraft sharing is that availability must often present a difficulty, but the actual experience of most groups is that the problem turns out to be under-use.

Let us imagine a group with six pilots, all of whom intend to fly about fifty hours a year each. This implies a total usage of 300 hour a year. In the event, some fail to fly anything like that and the actual usage runs out at only 175 hours a year. That does terrible things to the figures, so the group finds that the actual cost of operating the aircraft *per hour* greatly exceeds the estimates. With the group strapped for cash, maintenance is left undone and you find the aircraft flight log full of little warnings to say that the brakes are binding, there is interference on the radio and a bit of an oil leak. This may tend to discourage some partners from using the aircraft even as much as they did, and things go from bad to worse. Indeed, I have belonged to groups where years went by without some members of the group flying the aircraft at all. They still paid their monthly standing order and thought – no doubt – that they were doing their partners some sort of a favour by paying for something which they never used. Such people need to face up to the fact that they ought to sell their share and make room for more active aviators, because a 'sleeping partner' is making the per-hour cost of flying higher than it should be for those who actually use the aircraft. In my view, it is useful to have some sort of an arrangement within a group that the monthly fixed cost includes an amount in respect of perhaps two hours' flying per month *whether this is actually flown or not*. This does tend to prod partners into either using the aircraft or getting out.

As can be seen from the advertisements, the costs of aircraft sharing tends to vary with the size and complexity of the aircraft. Another significant cost determinant is the location at which the aircraft is based. At one end of the scale you will find many a light aeroplane operating off a farm strip and kept in a barn, while at the other end are the aircraft hangared at busy regional airports. The storage costs and landing fees can vary between next to nothing for the one up to around £5000 per annum for the other. Typical costs (in 2005) for a two-seat training type are around £5000 for a share, £40 per month and £40 per flying hour wet (i.e. including fuel). So if you fly 25 hours per year it will cost you £58·80 per hr. and if you fly 50 hours per year the hourly cost will work out at £49·60. Admittedly these figures ignore the use of capital tied up in the initial cost and take no account of depreciation, although this should not be significant with a well-maintained aircraft. Even so, these figures are substantially more attractive than those associated with the cost of hiring from a flying school.

What is equally important is the question of availability. Flying schools are often reluctant to hire out aircraft for much more than half a day at a time. Even where they are, they usually require you to pay for a minimum of perhaps three hours per day, whether these are actually flown or not. Given that most pilots get most satisfaction from going places in an aircraft – ideally for several days at a time – and given that they (or at least their passengers) may be averse to a holiday where at least three hours a day are spent airborne, the deal offered by the flying school makes little sense. On the other hand, most groups allow their members to take the aircraft away for days on end with no penalty. After all, a usage of 350 hours per year would be seen as good going by most groups. Nonetheless, this still represents only about 4% of the 8760 hours in a year, and the remaining 96% of the aircraft's time is spent waiting for another pilot to come along and take it flying.

Another bonus of group ownership is that it will get you intimately involved with the business of maintaining and operating an aircraft, and while so doing you are likely to form friendships with some of the other partners because of your common interests. That said, there are of course some groups which are best avoided. As with all partnerships, it is much easier to get in than out – and it is when the going gets difficult that relationships get tested. In some cases they will be found unequal to the situation and there will be much trouble and strife, which is not what you joined for. Before joining a group, check for the following:

> 1. A well-maintained aircraft with an up-to-date technical log showing consistent and conscientious care, and all Airworthiness Directives complied with.

> 2. A sensible and practical partnership agreement and set of rules. Make sure that there are clear arrangements for the majority to compel a partner to sell his/her share in the event of a falling-out, and that the group has the right to approve any prospective new partner.

A typical insurance schedule. Are the geographical limits and the limits of liability acceptable to you? In a group will the Captain at the time or the group as a whole pay the Excess?

3. Check the details of the insurance policy to make sure that they are appropriate and acceptable to you. In the event of a claim, who is responsible for paying any excess?

4. Read the aircraft journey log usually kept on board and filled in by pilots at the end of their trips. It may tell you much about how and when the aircraft is used, what defects occur, and whether there is animosity within the group.

5. If – as is often the case – there is one member who runs the group, judge whether he/she is someone you can trust to deal fairly, competently and responsibly with group matters.

6. Ask around. Speak to current (and if possible past) members.

A barn makes the cheapest form of undercover storage

A hangar. Usually expensive, but often the most convenient storage

Mutual Flying

Mutual Flying

Chapter 2

An Extra Resource

Mutual flying has always been a common means of practice in the military but it is not often met with in the world of private aviation. Which is not all that surprising, considering that mutual flying does not form any part of any CAA or JAA PPL syllabus. Nor does it present as obvious a source of income to a flying school as does dual training. Not for one moment do I advocate "mutual" as a substitute for dual training, but I do believe that it has a very valuable role to play in private flying as a complement to dual instruction.

There is one major difference between private flying and military flying. This is the crucial factor – from the pilot's point of view, at least – that the private pilot's flying is entirely at his or her expense whilst the fortunate service pilot soars about the sky entirely at the expense of the taxpayer and gets paid for it to boot! So a form of practice which costs less is always of particular interest to the private pilot, and mutual flying offers a very cost-effective way of improving your skills.

Mutual flying needs to be seen as an alternative to solo practice rather than as an alternative to dual training. Suppose, for example, you decide that an hour's forced-landing practice is what you really need. Out of that hour you will spend perhaps ten minutes taxying and perhaps twenty minutes transitting between the airfield and the various sites which you choose for your practices. So out of your hour you will be unlikely to spend more than 30 minutes engaged in actual PFLs. Now suppose that instead you get hold of another pilot also interested in forced-landing practice and you go off for, say, an hour and a half. You will still spend ten minutes taxying and probably a half-hour transitting. But now two of you will share fifty minutes of PFL practice. In the first instance, you had half an hour's practice at a cost of one hour's solo hire. In the second instance you had 25 minutes practice at a cost of 45 minutes (half of 1·5 hours) solo hire. On a financial basis alone you are winning, but this crude calculation ignores the benefit of watching other pilots carrying out a practice, monitoring their actions, second-guessing their judgements and learning from their mistakes.

If mutual flying makes sense as a cost-effective and beneficial alternative to solo practice of aircraft handling procedures, it makes even more sense when used for navigation. The private pilot is used to a regime where he or she flies solo all the time. Even when there is an instructor in the right-hand seat, most of the session is spent in that condition where the instructor specifically states that "You have control"; the student continues as if in sole charge with the instructor usually observing and commenting but almost never assisting. If the instructor takes over, the roles are reversed. The student then becomes the observer and would not dream of assisting unless specifically asked.

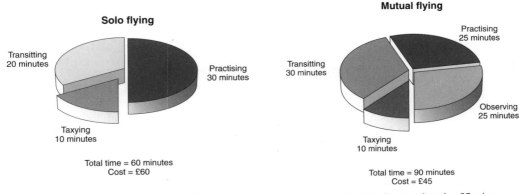

Solo flying will give you 30 mins practice for £60.

Mutual gives you 25 mins practice plus 25 mins observing for £45

In most commercial flying, however, aeroplanes are flown by crews. Much time is rightly spent these days in training the crew to work as a proper team (this is the world of Crew Resource Management, or CRM) and definitely not as a group of two or three individuals where one performs virtually all the functions leaving the others watching – suitably impressed no doubt – and holding themselves in readiness to take over if asked. Those days are long gone, and nowadays the roles are shared out in a defined manner. Each person has specific duties at any given time, but also has a general duty to monitor the actions of the other(s). Excess of workload is always a major source of danger in flying, and forgetting some vital action is another. A multi-person crew working well as a team is going to be well set-up to cope with both these dangers.

What demonstrably makes for greater safety in commercial flying can do the same for private flying, and this is very apparent when it comes to cross-country work. Most newly qualified PPLs face considerable difficulty in coping with trips outside their own well-loved and familiar local area. Their navigation test, which formed an important and memorable part of their training and skill test, is now somewhat behind them. At that time they were mothered around the route with a flying instructor having to approve the nav plot, the weather and all the arrangements. Recently qualified PPLs wishing to hire flying-club aircraft for a solo navigation trip away from the local area may receive some support, advice and encouragement from a flying school, but equally they may not. It all depends on the degree of enlightenment of the school and how much free time they have at that particular moment. After all, as a solo hirer you are not actually paying for anything other than the aircraft. Advice, encouragement, monitoring and so on are then on a purely grace-and-favour basis. If you are contemplating the trip in a privately owned aircraft, there may well be absolutely no backup available and consequently you will be entirely on your own.

You can therefore see that it is something of a giant leap for the low-hour PPL to embark on a solo cross-country unless the flying school or club is unusually supportive. Hence the advantages of flying a mutual trip are considerable. If the other pilot is more experienced than you, this extra experience will assist matters greatly – particularly if the other pilot is already familiar with the particular route. However, even if both pilots are only recently qualified and unfamiliar with the route, the advantages of flying as a team of two (as commercial pilots usually do, remember) are very substantial. Provided that you organise yourselves as a team, you are going to find that you are more effective as such than either one of you would be alone.

Who does what?

Officially, of course, the Captain is the sole pilot and anyone else on board a single pilot aircraft is a passenger, even if qualified as a pilot. However, that does not forbid the Captain from accepting some unofficial assistance provided that it is understood that the Captain is solely responsible for all aspects of the conduct of the flight. So let's assign two job titles to the members of our team. One will be "Captain" (Capt) and the other "Unofficial Assistant" (Asst). Capt. takes responsibility for all that goes on while accepting a helping hand from Asst. So at any point in the flight there must no possibility of doubt between the two of you as to which one is Captain. While the usual arrangement will be for one of you to remain as Captain throughout a particular flight, there is no reason why you should not swap roles during a flight always providing that you are both in no possible doubt as to when such a change has taken place. It is very similar to the position where an instructor hands over control to a student. "You have control" – "I have control", are the time honoured phrases to meet this occasion and if you are going to change captaincies during a flight you must be at least as formal and definite as this so as to ensure that no one is in any doubt. Something like, "You are now Captain" – "I am now Captain", is called for.

Captain and unofficial assistant discuss their next flight

When you are Captain, you must not allow deference to your companion or an unwillingness to tread on toes to interfere with your ensuring that the flight is conducted in as safe and responsible manner as possible. If you lose confidence in Asst.'s contribution then you must reject the assistance and do whatever you personally think the position calls for. Consider Asst.'s advice by all means, but in the end all judgements and decisions are yours.

When you are Unofficial Assistant you must remember that you are not in charge and officially are not even a crew member. If you think that you ought to be empowered to take over the captaincy on demand, for example because you own the aircraft or you have considerably more experience, you must negotiate this right to take over on demand before start up. The last thing that you want is a dispute as to who is Captain when an emergency springs up.

Having agreed your formal relationship, you can next consider the practicalities. The usual division of tasks is for one of you to do the handling while the other does the navigation and radio and it is probably simplest if the Captain does the handling. There may be some other tasks to be shared out and these should be discussed and agreed in advance. Two tasks fall to both of you – or all of you if there are more than two pilots on board – because this is a game that can be played by more than two pilots if so agreed beforehand. The first is lookout and it can be a good idea to award 'points' or some other such motivation to whoever first sees each aircraft that comes into view.

The second task is to monitor the activities of the other pilot(s). This is an activity that has come of age under the Cockpit Resources Management techniques that have so transformed the safety of civil air transport. The technique starts from the recognition that everybody, be they ever so skilled and experienced, makes mistakes quite frequently. Pilot error based accidents usually result from a chain of mistakes made by a crew culminating in disaster and if the chain can be broken before disaster strikes little or no harm will be the outcome. Primed with the recognition that everybody is fallible, crews are set to monitoring each other's performance throughout each flight. It is not only permissible for a co-pilot to monitor the

"500ft to go."

captain's activities, it is positively expected. While it is perhaps contrary to the Instructor/Student culture as we know it for the Student to point out to the Instructor that he has forgotten to switch the fuel pump off on climbing through 1,000ft, that would be a co-pilot's positive duty in a multi crew situation where switching off the fuel pump was the Captain's task. Once both crew members accept that, being human, they are subject to unfortunate lapses from time to time, it becomes much easier for one to correct the performance of the other occasionally. This sort of activity leads on, where cockpit resource management works well, to a continuing discussion of how the flight is going and how the next phase of the flight is going to be handled. Just discussing these issues as you go along provokes more detailed thought and far better mutual understanding of what is in the other crew member's mind.

So in addition to getting on with your own activities, be they handling or navigation and radio, you should also be continually monitoring what the other person is doing, providing gentle reminders of anything that seems to have been overlooked or arguments against, where you have reservations about a proposed course of action. The addition of indications of approval and satisfaction where appropriate will do much to keep levels of stress or aggravation at a low level.

Learning to function as a team does not come easily or naturally to a pilot whose entire training and experience has been as a solo operator. You are therefore both going to find things difficult and strange at first. In my view the best approach is to act in the same way as commercial pilots would, even if it all seems unnecessarily formal. And this means saying out loud what you have previously said only to yourself. The whole basis of teamwork is communication, and communication between the occupants of a light aircraft is almost entirely by speech. Therefore you must keep speaking even where previously you have habitually remained strong and silent.

Keep Communicating

Throughout the flight, therefore you should keep talking. You are reaching the top of your climb to cruising level:

> Asst "500ft to go"
>
> Capt "500ft"
>
> Capt "Level 50 coming up. I'm levelling out."
>
> Asst "The cruise heading is 283"
>
> Capt "283"
>
> Capt runs through FREDA checks and OP monitors.
>
> Capt "What's the next waypoint?"
>
> Asst "North abeam Alchester. We should be there in eight minutes. We should be tracking about two miles south of the river Avon and we are abeam Alchester when we cross the motorway."
>
> Capt "OK. Where do we make the next radio call?"
>
> Asst "In two minutes time I'm going to ask Hitheravon if we can go to Scanborough Radar so that they can give us a Radar Information Service past Alchester."

And so it continues for the rest of the sortie. Each pilot is continually telling the other what he is doing and what he is going to do next. When a pilot is not "telling" he is "asking", so that each is continually updated on the progress of the flight. On no account should you imagine, for instance, that your job is, say, simply to fly the heading, hold the height and make sure that all the instruments remain in the green sectors. You are listening to the Asst's radio calls and the replies, checking the read-backs and checking that the clearances are being complied with. You are also keeping an eye on the progress of the navigation and generally doing at least in your head all the things which you would have being doing if this had been a solo trip. If you are the Asst, you are probably working harder than the handling pilot while in the cruise. Nonetheless, relieved as you are of the what cruising yachtsmen call the "tyranny of the tiller", you have much more spare capacity for your radio and navigation duties than you would have if you had the handling to see to as well. This means that you should have a much better chance of getting the radio and navigation right than you would have had on a solo trip. Use some of that spare capacity to watch over the Capt, even in the cruise when there is not all that much for the latter to do. Are FREDA checks being carried out every ten minutes? When should the tanks be changed? Does the heading indicator correspond with the magnetic compass? Is the correct heading being flown? Is the correct level being maintained?

In the landing and take-off phases, the Asst's monitoring duties become all the more important. The Capt now has his or her work really cut out, and it will be all too easy to forget some vital point. It is *your* duty, just as much as the Capt's, to make sure that none of these get overlooked. Most important of all must be the airspeed, and there is much to recommend the commercial and military practice of having the non-handling pilot calling out the airspeed on take-off and on the approach.

While all this may sound unnecessarily formal, you should at the start at least of flying mutually with a new partner reject the temptation of leaving out what may seem to be a series of unnecessary communications beneath each other. It's far, far better to have too much of this than not enough. In time you may become used to each other's ways. Possibly you may then dispense with some of the formalities, but even here remember that accident reports of all sorts – whether aeronautical or not – are full of accounts of how A assumed that B had done something essential because that was what B always did. So A perceived no need to check on this occasion that B had done whatever it was that ought to have been done. The reports often go on to explain how on this particular and unique occasion B had departed from a lifetime's habit.

By flying as a team in this way, two pilots can perform with a good deal more competence than either could on their own. So this is a very good way of improving your individual ability. If, for example, you can get yourself around some new and unfamiliar route as a member of a team of two, you could probably do it next time on your own if you wanted to.

Two Buts

Mutual flying is a very valuable and cost-effective way for a private pilot to build ability and confidence. BUT there are two important caveats:

1. Don't confuse mutual flying with two or more of you just sharing a flight. In this much more common mode, two or more pilots go off together for the sake of sharing the cost and perhaps for a bit of company. One of them takes on the role of "pilot" for a leg and the other(s) more or less let him or her get on with it apart from giving the odd spot of assistance on an *ad hoc* and unstructured basis. This is not mutual flying as I mean it. To meet my definition, there has to be a declared and agreed intention to act as a team with a clear division of primary duties and a mutual understanding that each is expected to monitor the other throughout the flight.

2. Never confuse mutual flying with dual training. Especially on a handling practice flight, it is easy for the handling pilot to slip into the role of student while the non-handling pilot unconsciously becomes the "instructor". This is the simple result of habitude. With your entire experience of flying with two pilots being that of one playing the role of instructor and the other of student it is difficult to adopt an entirely different mode. Remember therefore that if the agreement is that the handling pilot does the handling and the non-handling pilot does the radio, the handling pilot must resist the habit of a lifetime and not change frequencies nor make calls without prior permission. Likewise, the non-handling pilot should not take over the handling unless this is first mutually agreed. The only exception to this is where the non-handling pilot is the captain and – probably because of some perceived emergency – takes control. Because this is hopefully an unlikely event, it is all the more important that the captain makes it crystal-clear at the time that he or she is taking over. If possible, it will greatly help if the reason can be explained.

On no account should you let the detail develop into a disorganised and dangerous jolly. I know of one handling pilot carrying out a PFL from overhead an airfield, desperate not to lose face in front of the three other friends on board. Consequently he stretched and stretched the glide towards the threshold so that the other pilot, in desperation, pushed open the throttle with the airspeed just above stalling, at a height of about five feet and some fifty yards to go to the threshold. Of course, the handling pilot should have abandoned the attempt at 100ft or so, but nonetheless the other pilot's surprise action in suddenly opening the throttle wide was very dangerous – as events were to show. The sudden application of 180hp to an aircraft just above stalling speed caused an immediate torque-roll in which the airframe tried to rotate around the engine. The wingtip struck the ground but luckily one of the pilots (nobody is too sure which one) managed to recover control just in time. It could have very easily ended up so much worse, so don't get carried away and don't behave as though you are the instructor unless you actually are.

Manoeuvers –Practising your Scales

Manoeuvers
– Practising your Scales

Chapter 3

General

The PPL syllabus includes manoeuvres such as turns, climbs, descents, climbing and descending turns, stalls and incipient spins. However, there is a whole range of manoeuvres suitable for non-aerobatic aircraft which if practised and mastered will improve a pilot's ability and confidence in handling. Some go beyond the PPL syllabus, although they are all made up of the fundamental ingredients which form part of basic training. All are well worth practising. The PPL-syllabus manoeuvres, together with those that follow, might be regarded as exercises similar to a musician's scales. All musicians, be they never so consummate, will practice scales over and over again. Scales are the building bricks of musical skill, and air exercises are the building bricks of the pilot's skills. So learn how to do them and then, like the consummate musician, practice them frequently – always striving for perfection and never accepting that near enough is good enough.

When first learning these manoeuvres, take a good instructor along until both of you are confident that you can recover properly from anything which goes wrong. Finding a "good" instructor is not going to be all that easy. An ex-military instructor will certainly have the necessary experience, and a civilian interested and qualified in aerobatic instruction should also fit the bill. Unfortunately there are many flying instructors at schools today whose experience of any sort of aircraft handling beyond the requirements of the PPL syllabus is virtually nil. A civil flying instructor's training is limited to teaching the PPL syllabus, and an extra rating is required to gain approval to teach aerobatics. Without this, an instructor will almost certainly have insufficient experience to be a "good" instructor for our purposes.

Prior instruction

Exercises which form part of the PPL syllabus may not require any further instruction if you are in good practice on the particular aircraft type. However, if you are flying an aircraft on which you have not previously executed the PPL exercises, you should take an instructor along until you are both confident of your ability. All the exercises which go beyond the PPL syllabus call for dual instruction to start with.

Always carry out your HASELL checks and don't let the speed exceed Va (maximum manoeuvring speed) for your aircraft. If by mistake you should do so, bear in mind that full control deflection will now overstress your aircraft – so be gentle if you would prefer to keep the wings on.

Manoeuvres

Stalls

The conventional basic-training stall usually comprises cutting the power while flying straight and level, and maintaining height and direction with the controls as the speed falls off until the stall is reached. The necessity of keeping the slip ball in the middle throughout both the stall and the recovery should be stressed by the instructor. Modern trainers are much more forgiving than most other types and checking a dropping wing at the point of the stall with aileron will probably do the trick without any unpleasantness. There are many other types, however, where this technique may flick you into a spin before you can say "Always remember to use rudder to check a dropping wing at low speeds". Practising your scales is all about repeatedly doing the right thing so that it becomes instinctive. You obviously need to practice the *correct* action (checking a dropping wing with opposite rudder) even if you are flying a basic trainer which is able to indulge any lack of skill or awareness in this department.

Basic training should also have taught you the stall in various other conditions, including the approach configuration and in a descending low-power turn. This is of course the classic loss-of-control scenario on the turn from base leg to finals. Unfortunate victims of this syndrome are so preoccupied with lining up, dealing with the radio and looking out – or perhaps they are simply tired and not thinking properly – that the airspeed and degree of bank do not receive the essential monitoring which is so vital at this point. You practised incipient stalls in this condition (at a safe height) in your basic training, and you need to keep on practising them for as long as you keep flying. If you fly a four-seater, see the passage at the end of this chapter.

Spins

The current PPL syllabus includes incipient spins and recovery from them, but does not teach the actual spin and recovery. The thinking goes that it is more useful to know how to recognise the onset of the spin, and how to recover from that, than to involve yourself in the full spin and its recovery. The controversy on this subject continues, and one telling argument advanced by the proponents of the School of No Spinning is that there have been cases of students – sometimes with instructors – practising spins, failing to recover and coming to grief. On the other hand, many instructors believe strongly that a pilot who has never experienced a spin and its recovery will always be in fear of the unknown, and will consequently lack confidence when flying anything but the most gentle of manoeuvres. Furthermore the non-spinning pilot will be in considerable danger later if converting to any but the most benign of types. Many such instructors therefore include spins and their recovery as part of the PPL training, although it is no longer a required part of the syllabus.

If you now have a PPL and have never been taught spinning and spin recovery, it is entirely up to you whether you seek further training. If you do, make sure that the task is undertaken in an aircraft type which is cleared for spinning, a particular aircraft which is regularly used for spinning and an instructor who regularly teaches spins and their recovery. The point is that the occasional aircraft may have an undetected rigging fault making it difficult to recover from a spin, and some instructors may not be sufficiently proficient in the necessary technique to be absolutely reliable.

If you have learned or elect to learn spins and recovery and you have access to an aircraft which is regularly spun, you should include the actual spin as one of your regular practices. You will find that being in practice will give you confidence and may just save the day if one day you should fail to recover from a spin at the incipient stage.

Sideslipping

The sideslip is useful way of losing height without increasing speed. In aircraft of an earlier generation not fitted with flaps, it was the standard means of increasing the rate of descent on the approach. Some aircraft are not cleared for sideslipping if the flaps have been lowered, usually because lowering flaps reduces or confuses the airflow over the tail control surfaces, and some aircraft are not cleared for sideslipping in any circumstances. Clearly you should start by consulting the POH/FM.

Assuming your aircraft is suitably cleared, this manoeuvre is well worth perfecting. It is useful for losing extra height if power-off, wheels down and flaps are not getting you down fast enough (in a misjudged glide approach for instance). It is also handy for inducing airflow with a sideways element over the aircraft, which is sometimes useful in getting an open door shut or in dealing with fire when airborne. Sideslipping is also a good way of keeping the runway threshold in sight on finals in aircraft types where the view forward is poor, and in the standard wing-down crosswind landing when the final part of the approach is flown in this way.

In the sideslip you fly with crossed controls and this creates extra form drag. Because it is usually seen as an approach manoeuvre, pilots commonly believe that it is for use only when gliding. However, in most types you can sideslip straight and level if you want to, or even in the climb. Indeed, every time you find yourself flying with the ball off-centre you are in fact sideslipping. A valuable way of squeezing an extra knot or so out of cruise power is to pay careful attention to getting the ball in the middle. If it is not, you will be creating extra drag and that can only lead to less airspeed.

To sideslip, all you need to do is to fly out of balance with the ball out to one side, keeping the wings in the attitude you require by applying the appropriate degree of opposite aileron. If you feed in full rudder deflection, you will achieve the maximum amount of sideslip for that particular airspeed and create a significant degree of extra drag in the process. You will need to maintain your airspeed. That can be achieved either by adding power – if your intention is to maintain height – or by increasing your angle of descent if you are trying to steepen your approach without increasing speed.

Some aircraft can be sideslipped much more radically than others, and the determinant is usually the amount of rudder authority possessed by the aircraft.

When you are first taught to sideslip, especially if you have never been taught wing-down crosswind landings, the whole manoeuvre seems to be fraught with risk. You have had drummed into you over and over again that flying with crossed controls is dangerous because any stall is liable to turn into a spin. In actual fact that is perfectly true, but to spin you first have to stall. So when sideslipping, it is essential to pay particular attention to the risk of stalling and monitor your speed even more carefully. The loss-of-control accidents which start from a stall with crossed controls almost invariably involve **inadvertent** crossing of the controls. The pilot has become absorbed in something else – typically lining up with the runway in a crosswind which has carried the aircraft over to the dead side – and has ceased to monitor either airspeed or balance of the controls. The pilot who intentionally enters a sideslip, however, is well aware of the crossed-controls condition and will monitor the airspeed with extra care because of this. There is no need to make an exaggerated increase in speed because of the crossed controls. In many aircraft no increase is necessary.

Sideslip can be applied in the turn, where the application of top rudder to create an out-of-balance turn will significantly increase the form drag. This "slipping turn" is a useful manoeuvre in a glide approach on to finals. The application of top rudder in this turn will produce substantial height loss. Alternatively, sideslipping can be used during a series of S-turns on finals to lose height. It is in the course of the turn on to final approach that you have (I hope) always been taught to be particularly careful to check that the turn is properly in balance – yet it is now suggested that you intentionally fly out of balance. So remember to be particularly careful in monitoring airspeed and angle of bank, and be prepared to return the ball to the middle while reducing the angle of attack of the wings if there should be any sign of an incipient stall

Slow flight

Exercise 10 of the PPL syllabus taught you slow flight whilst straight and level, climbing, descending and turning. The main purpose was to get you to recognise slow flight as a condition; to appreciate the differences in handling; and in most flight conditions other than take-off and landing, to impel you to raise the speed to something safer. However, the more advanced PPL will do well to become familiar with all aspects of slow flight and to practice it frequently.

Why?

Because you are going to need to know how to fly slowly but safely for precision landings and take-offs. Also because slow-flight practice at a safe height will keep you constantly close to the point of stall, and will increase your skills in recognising the incipient or actual stall in various conditions and in recovering from them.

In addition to the PPL manoeuvres, you would do well to practise Boxing the Horizon and Lazy Eights as slow-flight exercises. Both are described later in this chapter.

Steep turns

It is interesting to note that under FAA (United States) rules any turn where the angle of bank exceeds 60° is regarded as aerobatics and therefore not permitted unless both aircraft and pilot are cleared for them. However, as far as the JAA is concerned you can pile on as much angle of bank as you care to, although in practice there is a maximum angle which your aircraft can sustain in level flight which is dictated by the amount of power available. Two useful refinements of steep-turn practice are:

In the USA a turn of over 60° bank is classed as aerobatics and needs special training

1   While maintaining altitude in a steep turn, increase the bank and the aft loading on the yoke until the stall warning sounds. You will have done this as part of your basic training, and you will remember that you are investigating the high-speed stall. The stall warning tells you that you are approaching maximum angle of attack, although the ASI might lead you to think that the stall is a long way off.

2   Fly your steep turn with such precision that you encounter turbulence from your own slipstream as you fly once more through the airspace through which you were turning a little earlier. This is not as easy as it sounds, and is consequently highly rewarding when you do it.

Spiral dives

You will have done spiral dives as a PPL exercise. The inadvertent spiral dive usually results from an improperly executed steep turn, with insufficient attention being paid to maintaining the nose in the correct position in relation to the horizon. I often intentionally start my spiral dives from a steep turn so as to remind myself how easy it is to let the spiral develop unintentionally. It's not wise to try to recapture the steep turn from the spiral dive because this could easily overstress the aircraft. So stick to the conventional recovery of reducing power, levelling the wings and easing gently out of the dive.

Boxing the horizon

This is an exercise which involves a splendid range of continually varying control inputs, including rudder and power.

What you have to do is to describe a shape on the horizon with the nose of your aircraft. Most people start with a rectangle with the long side parallel with the horizon, but when you get bored with that you can graduate to any shape you fancy. A perfect circle for instance, is quite a challenge; if you can hack that with ease, you can always try writing your name. Start at about five or ten knots below Va, and when you are happy with your performance, try it again only slightly above stalling speed.

There are two common variants of boxing the horizon:

(a) wings level throughout and accepting a crossed-control condition in the horizontal movements, and

(b) wings banked as necessary, in which case the ball should be in the centre throughout.

Both are entertaining and educational. Generally I prefer the crossed-control method as having more to teach you, although at low speed you should certainly start by using the balanced-control technique. Flying with crossed controls close to stalling speed risks an incipient spin, so you need to be competent in recognising and recovering from this. You also need plenty of height for safety's sake. If anyone should suggest that the exercise is inherently dangerous and maybe even foolish, just remind them that the widely used wing-down method of crosswind landing comprises exactly the same condition: low speed and crossed controls. The only difference is that the crosswind landing is carried out at too low a height to give any hope of recovery if a spin should develop, whilst boxing the compass with wings level is carried out with plenty of height in hand.

In fact, the more you practice unusual manoeuvres of any sort (provided they are within your own and the aircraft's limitations and carried out at a safe height) the more proficient a pilot you are going to become. After all, any idiot can fly the cruise, but a pilot who is familiar with the aircraft's handling and responses throughout its entire flight envelope is going to be far better placed to cope with the nasty surprises which can always crop up in any aviator's career – even those dedicated to the cruise condition.

So let's describe a rectangle on the horizon with our nose. Do your HASELL checks and then proceed thus:

- ■ Establish yourself straight and level at your selected speed for the exercise, heading for a landmark.

- ■ Note the relationship of your nose to the horizon at this speed. This is your midway vertical reference. You are starting your exercise halfway up the left-hand side of your rectangle, and you are about to describe the upper half of the left-hand portion of it.

- ■ To do this, increase power (so as to maintain speed, which should not alter throughout the exercise). Then apply back pressure on the yoke and feed in a little anti-torque rudder.

- Continue up to the top of the left-hand side. The top should be less than where your nose would be in the normal climbing attitude.

- Now you have to traverse along the top side of your rectangle; and I will assume that this time we are doing the wings-level variant of the exercise. You will need to keep the back pressure on the yoke to keep the nose up by just the right amount, and you have to monitor your speed and perhaps make small power adjustments.

- Feed in right rudder and keep the wings level with opposite aileron. The rudder command should progress until you reach the stop.

- When at the end of your chosen traverse, centralise the rudder and the opposite aileron so that the ball is once more central.

- Now descend through the right-hand side of your rectangle by forward movement of the yoke, slight at first. Decrease power to maintain your chosen speed and feed in a little pro-torque rudder to balance the reduced power.

- Take the nose down to as much below the initial reference point as you were above it at the top of the rectangle.

- Check the downward progress and traverse to the left, finishing up exactly below your initial reference.

- Ease back on the yoke, apply power and anti-torque rudder until you arrive back where you started.

- Level out, reduce power and check balance.

Most pilots new to this exercise are a bit ragged at first but practice will make perfect. Remember to keep your control inputs small and always smooth.

The banked-wing variant is just the same except that when traversing you feed in bank for a rate-one turn, keeping the ball in the centre throughout the exercise.

Chandelle

This is a delightful manoeuvre, which is not aerobatic but is about as close to it as either birds or non-aerobatic pilots ever get. It comprises a climbing turn through 180°, starting at above cruising speed and finishing just above stalling speed.

The Chandelle

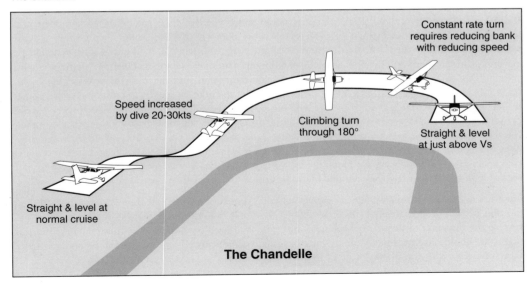

The Chandelle

Here's how you do it:

- As always, start with HASELL
- Establish yourself straight and level at normal cruise settings and speed, aligned with some linear ground feature such as a straight road. This will give you a reference for your 180° of turn. If there is no linear ground feature, use the sun. If there is neither a linear ground feature nor any sun, use your initiative. No power adjustment is required during the manoeuvre.
- Apply forward pressure on the yoke so as to enter a dive until the speed has increased by 20-30kts (subject to any relevant maximum speed limitations). Apply bank and simultaneously ease back progressively on the yoke so as to attain your maximum angle of bank of about 60° by the time you have completed 90° of the turn. For the remaining 90° of your turn you continue to increase progressively the pitch-up while you decrease progressively the angle of bank. As you finish the complete 180° of turn, you are close to the point of stall. Keep the ball in the middle throughout. Allow for the fact that as your speed reduces, your rate of turn increases. Since you should keep the rate of turn constant, you need to reduce the angle of bank progressively through the second half of the manoeuvre.
- The exercise calls for careful control inputs and a good awareness of energy management as you progressively convert speed into height. It also demonstrates most effectively the way your rate of turn increases with reducing speed unless you reduce your angle of bank. The chandelle forms a required part of the FAA Commercial Pilot's flight test in which you are required to show a good height gain, a smooth progression through the exercise and no actual stall at any point.

In the UK the chandelle is not part of any recognised flight test, which is perhaps a pity. Indeed, the manoeuvre is understood by many British pilots, particularly those involved in aerobatics, to be a rather more extensive procedure in which the events described above are followed by a continuation of the turn but with the pitch being reduced so that the aircraft swoops down from its zenith. At the bottom of the descent the turn is reversed and the aircraft restored to straight and level flight. This manoeuvre is also known as a "wingover". I do not recommend this version of the chandelle as a non-aerobatic exercise as it is easy to overdo the rate of descent and to exceed Va. Beginners sometimes forget, in the excitement of the moment, to close the throttle as the descent begins. This naturally leads in no time to excessive speed.

Remember that what you are creating in the second half of the wingover is a spiral dive. Remember also the standard recovery, which is first to close the throttle, if it is not already closed; level the wings with aileron, checking that you are keeping the ball in the middle; and then ease **gently** out of the dive.

Lazy eights

In the lazy eight you fly a figure-of-eight in plan view, varying your height as you do so. The manoeuvre is rather more difficult to describe than it is to fly, so take what follows in small steps until the procedure is clear. Begin with a turn through 180°, starting level at about 20kts less than Va. The power setting should be appropriate to this speed and the nose lined up on a distant mark such as the sun. The power setting remains constant throughout the manoeuvre. Start a gentle balanced turn and gradually raise the nose to a high point close to the stall as you pass through 90° of turn. Then lower the nose, so that by the time you pass through the 180° point you are back at your starting level but with the descent continuing. Do not let speed exceed Va in the descent. You then reverse the direction of the turn and allow the descent to continue to a low point. This should be the same amount below the horizon as you were formerly above it. You should reach this stage of the manoeuvre when your new direction of turn has taken you through the 90° point, so that your original reference mark is on your wing-tip. Continue the turn but now climb once more so that you recover your original level when you regain your original heading and are pointing once more at your reference mark.

You are now halfway through your lazy eight. Continue your turn in the same direction, raising and then lowering it back to level through the next 180° – by which time the mark will be directly behind you. Reverse the direction of turn, lower the nose and raise it to level once more over the final 180°. By this stage you should have regained your original heading, position, speed and height and have described a figure-of-eight on its side whether viewed in plan or elevation.

As your speed varies throughout the manoeuvre, so does the rate of turn. Appropriate adjustments therefore need to be made to the angle of bank. Start at around 12° and at the zenith of the climb, when your speed should have reduced to somewhere near the stall, you will then be turning far more quickly than when you began. As you pass through the 180° point you will have accelerated once more and now have to reverse your turn. Something around 30° of bank will be needed through this part of the procedure, when the speed is relatively high.

You should aim to end up at the original heading and height without having made any adjustment to the original power setting. If you failed to turn through the full 180° by the halfway point, you probably spent too short a time at low speed at the zenith.

If you habitually lose height in the manoeuvre, use a higher power setting throughout and *vice versa*.

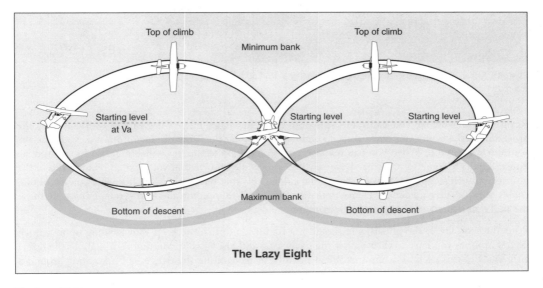

The Lazy Eight

Low-level flight

Low-level flight – by which I mean flight at little more than 500ft AGL – is always practised on take-off and landing and also often in the course of practice forced landings. There are two handling points to watch for. Firstly, you have not enough height in hand to recover from a spin, and precious little to recover from a stall. Secondly, low-level flight in high wind introduces the special danger of the pilot believing that the groundspeed is the same as the airspeed, when in fact it can be nothing of the sort.

To be a useful exercise, therefore, you really need a significant wind at the 500ft level, say 20kts or so. If the met man can't oblige on the day, you have my permission – at no charge – to use Everett's Artificial Wind, patent nearly applied for. Ideally this takes the form of a relatively slow-moving freight train. If you can't find one of these on the day, look for some other moving vehicle with a reasonably constant speed and direction. Ships can be useful and motorways are fertile ground, although they may present problems in identifying your particular target vehicle and usually replicate a wind of more like 60kts. Whatever you choose, the chosen target vehicle is used as your reference point. In effect it represents a stationary point on the ground in a high wind blowing in the opposite direction to the target's direction of travel (corrected if necessary for the effect of the actual wind on the day).

Everett's Artificial Wind. A useful device for simulating a 15kt surface wind

Regardless of whether you carry out this exercise in an actual high wind or the artificial one, the procedure is the same: you circle your chosen target, keeping the same distance from it as you describe your circle around it. When you can manage circles, move on to squares with the target in the middle. You will quickly come to recognize how easy it is to become absorbed in your spatial relationship to the target. So much so, in fact, that you forget the golden rule that navigating, which is what you are about, comes only second to aviating. Hence your first priority is to monitor airspeed – remaining well above the stall – and angle of bank, say 45° maximum.

Primed as you are to the pitfalls, you should not find it too difficult to keep your aviating up to scratch even if at times you have to throw away the navigating and just let your constant radius about the target go hang. But this exercise is most excellent practice in recognising the dangers of navigating around a ground-based target in strong winds, and accepting the vital priority which aviation must always have over navigation. Practice regularly and you will greatly reduce your chances of ending up one of those sad loss-of-control statistics which usually stem from the pilot forgetting the essential priority that aviating has over all other functions.

Incidentally, a useful opportunity for practice often arises when you are asked by air traffic to orbit in or near the circuit.

The Four-seat Flying Tiger

If you aircraft is a four-seater, practising stalls and incipient spins with just one or two aboard and no baggage may well lead you to believe that your particular aircraft is somehow bullet-proof in the loss-of-control department. You can slow it right down to the straight-and-level stall speed and haul on as much bank and aft stick pressure as you can, and it just won't bite you. Actually, the four-seat light aircraft can be a dangerous beast sometimes. It seems to be a gentle little thing, cute and friendly, and then one day turns into something much less forgiving. With two up and no baggage, your average four-seater is well into pussycat mode. This is because you have arranged the centre of gravity well forward, and there is often insufficient elevator authority at low speed and low power to overcome the forward C of G condition sufficiently for the aircraft to bite. If you want to see this sleepy moggy in its true tiger colours, you need to place the centre of gravity at the rear of the permitted range and then repeat the manoeuvre.

If you believe in education of the masses, the best bet is to fill all four seats with pilots – adding baggage if necessary so as to get the C of G at the rear of the range. The advantage of using aviators as ballast is that even those in the back seats get to encounter a glimpse of the tiger's jaws. Be the captain of this aircraft never so experienced, however, it is often difficult to persuade any pilots to occupy the rear seats for this exercise. Indeed, I must admit that I for one would not climb into the back seat with anyone but a pilot very capable indeed in light-aircraft handling. The whole point is that most four-seaters are **not** cleared for spinning, and those that are so cleared are not usually cleared for spinning with four up. This is precisely because of the extra difficulty in spin recovery with the C of G aft. It follows therefore that if the practice incipient-stall-in-approach-configuration should be allowed to become an actual stall, developing into a spin before anyone can so much as say "whoops", the four folk aboard will now find themselves in the interesting position of flying in an aircraft which is exceeding its permitted flight conditions. They are now test pilots all, and I sincerely hope that the handling pilot who allows this undesirable state of affairs to develop will be able to recover quickly and effectively from a spin with the centre of gravity well aft. You will realise that I am not recommending that you even think about doing this – let alone trying it out for real.

It's a curious fact that while volunteers for a four-seat trip to investigate incipient stalls in the approach configuration at altitude are almost as rare as rocking-horse manure, you will see fully loaded four-seaters arriving in great numbers at popular fly-ins. All of them are potential candidates for the incipient stall during the turn on to finals, but this time at about 500ft AGL. If you happen not to be the handling pilot on such a trip, you could do everybody a service by monitoring the ASI and angle of bank all the way from circuit height to touch-down.

If volunteers for the back seat are hard to come by, you can still get up there and count the tiger's teeth – and indeed you should. Load up the baggage compartment with well tied-down kit so as to get the centre of gravity fully aft within the permitted range. Make sure that you don't exceed the limits of C of G range, maximum all-up weight or the maximum permitted baggage compartment weight, and ensure that the load is properly distributed. If necessary, add some properly tied-down load in the back-seat area as well. Take a skilled instructor with you and go and find out what your aircraft is really like on the approach when fully laden with the C of G well aft. Take it to the edge of the stall, *but no further* in approach configuration, and also take it to the incipient spin when cleaned up. It's perfectly safe provided you watch the speed and angle of bank, but on most four-seaters it is now quite possible to take things to the edge and to catch a glimpse of your pussycat about to turn tiger.

Appreciating as you now do the true nature of your aircraft when fully laden, why not – when flying as handling pilot with four up – request one of your companions to monitor speed and angle of bank on the approach? It should at least quell some of the carefree but distracting chatter down finals.

The thing about four-seaters (and six-seaters even more so) is that we tend to practice our scales with only one or two POB and may not appreciate that the handling may be significantly different when the same aircraft is fully loaded. Pitch control is more sensitive, stalling speeds are higher and recovery from stalls and spins is more difficult. "Loss of control" is statistically one of the most common causes of light aircraft fatalities; not a few of these occur when the aircraft is fully laden and inevitably less foolproof than when less so.

In my own experience I know of a sad case where a fully loaded four-seater took off in unexceptional conditions, entered a departure stall at about 300ft and finished up in a heap. The front-seat occupants were badly injured and the rear-seat passengers killed. The pilot was used to flying the aircraft lightly laden. He perhaps made no allowance for the more sensitive pitch control with the C of G well aft and achieved after take-off an unsustainable nose-up attitude from which he failed to recover in time.

Take-offs

Take-offs

Much of your PPL training was taken up with good old circuits and bumps. So you may regard the award of your PPL as a licence to forget all that elementary stuff and get up in the sky and do whatever it is that the grown-up pilots do.

Well, whatever else grown-up pilots may do, you may be sure that the more competent ones keep up their circuit work. "Why is this?" you ask. And the answer is twofold:

- Circuit work is more of a challenge than most other things in the range of aviation activities available to most of us. If you leave out aerobatics or formation flying, circuits are where the private pilot is most challenged in the basics of actual aircraft handling. More challenge means more satisfaction – when you get it right, that is.

- Around 70 or 80% of flying accidents occur in the take-off or landing phases, so it must make sense to keep in constant practice in these demanding flying activities.

If you keep flying at all, it is going to be fairly difficult to avoid carrying out one take-off and one landing per trip. But don't let yourself think that these are sufficient practice in themselves. So, although it may seem like going back to school again, it's well worth putting in time on circuit practice throughout your flying life.

The standard take-off

You have been taught and will have remembered the basics of the standard take-off, to wit:

- Check the approach for other aircraft before entering the runway.
- Line up and pick a reference point ahead.
- Check RPM for full power and the ASI for rising airspeed on the take-off run.
- Keep straight, and on the centreline if there is one.
- Take the weight off the nosewheel or lift the tailwheel as soon as you reasonably can, unless the POH/FM advises otherwise.
- Rotate and lift-off at the speed specified in the POH/FM.
- Fly straight and level above the runway until climbing speed approaches and then ease into the climb.
- Maintain climbing speed and direction.

You may or may not have been taught the further refinements following. If not, and subject to the POH/FM saying anything to the contrary, I would recommend that you adopt them.

The Captain's Brief

In commercial flying it is standard practice (and almost certainly a laid-down requirement in the company's Operations Manual) for the aircraft captain to brief the crew before take-off. Depending on the aircraft and the circumstances, the brief might be along the following lines:

"Rotate speed will be 70kts. In the event of an engine failure or other emergency during the take-off when the aircraft is still on the runway, I shall close the throttle and stop the aircraft on the runway. If airborne and there is sufficient runway space left, I shall endeavour to land and stop on the runway. If there is insufficient runway space, I shall land in the most suitable space available. I shall ask you to assist by opening the doors during the approach to the forced landing, and also ask you all to assume the brace position before landing. Are there any questions?"

For multi-engined and larger aircraft there will be more to the captain's brief, but this need not concern us here.

You may think that this is all very fine and large for an airline pilot (especially if he happens to have the senior training captain sitting in the jump seat) but entirely over the top in respect of a private pilot. I would respectfully suggest, however, that you have a look at the practice of glider pilots. These folk operate aircraft a good deal simpler than those of the average PPL and yet they adopt virtually the same practice. The glider pilot's litany, recited just before starting the take-off (signalling "take-up slack") begins:

"In the event of a cable break…"

So if it's good enough for both glider pilots and for airline pilots, it must surely be good for PPLs as well.

What the captain's brief is all about is mind-set. When you take-off in an aircraft, you suddenly change not only the environment but also the workload. It takes most pilots a bit of time to get up to speed at this point, and even in a normal take-off you may often notice yourself or A N Other getting a little behind the aircraft. By the time you have climbed the first thousand feet or so, you will probably settled down and will be feeling more on top of things. In the interim, however, you are not in the best condition to handle effectively that most testing of eventualities; the engine failure (or cable break) after take-off. This is, after all, one of those emergencies where time is of the essence and you simply cannot afford to spend precious seconds working out what to do next. If the engine fails at 200ft and you have already let the airspeed fall 15kts below the climbing speed, only quick and positive action will save the day.

The main purpose of the brief is to remind the captain and the crew that engine failures (or cable breaks) *do* occur on take-off sometimes. So having the appropriate remedies set out in everyone's mind just in case is manifestly a Good Thing. If you are flying solo, that is absolutely no reason for omitting the brief. You simply have the privilege of choice as to whether you recite it out loud or to yourself. Incidentally, it's part of a test pilot's training always to assume that every take-off is going to end in engine failure.

The Engine Run up

I am indebted to Captain Eric Thurston, of Stapleford Flying Centre – a vastly experienced pilot and a licensed aircraft engineer to boot – for the following tip.

Line-up and then hold at power check setting before take-off

Research has shown that when you open an aircraft engine up to full power from taxying and carrying out power checks, it is insufficiently warmed up to develop its full output. The loss of power occurs because of excessive clearances between the piston rings and the cylinder walls, and these are caused by the relative coolness of the piston rings and cylinders. When these are at or close to their design temperature for full-power operation, the machinery is in its optimum state. So when you open up the throttle after taxying out and carrying out power checks, you have an engine which may easily be developing some 5% less than full power. By the time you have got airborne and climbed a hundred feet or so, the engine temperatures may well have reached their optimum and the engine will then be genuinely capable of delivering 100%. However, the take-off run and initial climb are when you really want full power available, not twenty or thirty seconds after first opening the throttle. The remedy is to line up on the runway, apply the brakes and open the throttle to power-check RPM. Hold this setting for about twenty seconds and only then release the brakes and gently open the throttle for the remainder of the range. In this way, you will get genuine full power when you most need it. You will also be helping to prolong your engine life by reducing the degree of thermal shock which always tends to be present on opening up from idle to full throttle.

Of course you can't always loiter around on the runway for twenty seconds if you are going to obstruct others on the approach or waiting for take-off clearance, but when the opportunity is there you should seize it. You can put the twenty-second pause to good use by checking the freedom of the controls, checking the runway heading against the magnetic compass and HI indications and noting the direction and strength of the wind. This could be useful information if this is the day for your engine failure after take-off. That apart, you were going to apply a bit of into-wind aileron during the take-off run and you were going to allow for drift on your climb-out, weren't you?

The power reduction to climb settings

A further point of engine handling arises with relation to the reduction in power from take-off to climb settings. A simple trainer may well use the same setting for both conditions, but even in this case there are many who advocate a small reduction in power for the climb-out where full noise is not essential. This will save unnecessarily stressing the engine. On more complex power units there is often a difference between take-off and climb settings. The climb setting amounts to a "maximum continuous" rating, while the take-off setting should be used for a limited period only – typically a maximum of five minutes.

Insofar as aircraft engines are prone to fail at all, and luckily they are not, a favourite time for them to chose to misbehave is when an adjustment is made to the power settings. This is a time when different stresses are suddenly introduced into the engine, and one of these may be the proverbial straw which breaks the camel's back of some component which is in any case getting close to collapse. If therefore you are, as a prudent pilot, half-expecting engine failure during your take-off, you should be particularly awake whenever you change throttle or RPM settings. So if you can make your power reduction while there is still space in which to put the aircraft down on the runway again in the event of an engine failure, it can often make sense to do just that. You can then reduce power to the climb setting as soon as you have reached climbing speed. Alternatively, if there is insufficient runway left to land back on by the time you have reached climbing speed, consider when would be the best time to reduce power. If maintaining maximum urge for another thirty seconds will take you clear of the housing estate beneath, it could be a good idea to postpone the business of power reduction until then.

Retractables

If you fly an aircraft with retractable undercarriage, your take-off procedure is almost certainly going to include raising the wheels. Probably this will involve no more than flicking an electrical switch, but things are not always that simple.

The 1936 Avro Anson Mk 1 – the RAF's first aeroplane with a retractable undercarriage – gave its unfortunate crew the considerable chore of winding up the wheels by hand. It took 119 turns of the operating handle to do the business, and a crew which incurred the flight commander's displeasure might be sent on a circuit detail with specific instructions to raise and lower the undercarriage fully on each circuit.

Early marks of Spitfire had the undercarriage operating pump-handle on the right-hand side of the cockpit. This meant that on take-off the pilot had to transfer the control column from his right to his left hand while operating the pump, and then change hands again afterwards. Any pilot new to the Spitfire was very likely to reveal his unfamiliarity with the type at this juncture by allowing some unintended departures to occur from the smooth climb-out. Thus was the novice revealed to all watching the take-off.

Manually raising the undercarriage of the earlier Fournier RF series, on the other hand, is carried out by just one sweep of the operating lever. However, matters are so arranged that you need one hand to hold the locking handle in the released position; another to operate the retraction lever; and, unfortunately, a third to keep control of the aircraft. To add to your problems, the retraction lever – in the course of its 170° sweep from forward to aft – often ends up inserted well into the unwary pilot's trouser leg. Consequently the Fournier has been described as an ideal aircraft for any pilot with three arms and one leg.

Leaving aside the possible vagaries of some aircraft types, we still have to resolve the contentious issue of just when you should raise the wheels. There is always a temptation to do so at the earliest possible opportunity. Indeed there are some aviators whose favoured means of transition from being ground-borne to airborne is simply to continue the ground run until flying speed is reached and then remove the intervening undercarriage by retracting it. Such a procedure looks very smart, but actually it is anything but. You may well get away with it for a while – but one day there will come a gust, or a sudden lull in the headwind, and you will descend fractionally. Now if the clearance between your propeller tips and the runway is two feet and you descend one foot and eleven inches, all may be well. But if you descend two feet and one inch… well, instead of being Ace of the Base you will undoubtedly be Twit of the Year.

There is an argument to the effect that once airborne your wheels whilst down contribute nothing but drag and plenty of it. Getting them neatly tucked away is going to give you a quicker and safer climb-out – so you should raise the undercarriage as soon as it safe to do so. Alternatively, in the view of many, the earliest safe point at which the wheels may be raised is when you have reached climbing speed and have begun the climb.

But there are some (and I am one of them) who argue that in cases where there is plenty of runway available, this is too soon to retract. Our view is that the wheels should be left down at least until you have passed the point where you could glide back on to the runway in the event of an engine failure after take-off. After all, if you are going to be returning to the runway, you will want maximum drag so as to get down again in the minimum distance. So you are going to want your wheels lowered for the touch-down. Even if an engine failure is liable to result in an off-airfield forced landing, you are probably going to be better off with the wheels down when you touch down. Admittedly a touch-down on water or very soft ground would probably be less damaging with the gear up, but on virtually any other terrain you need the wheels down so as to absorb as much as possible of the initial impact.

Given that the greatest likelihood of engine failure occurs when you change the throttle and pitch settings from maximum to climb, it therefore seems prudent to delay the raising of the undercarriage until either:

■ Completion of the reduction to climb setting for the engine, or

■ Passing the point where a glide back on to the runway would be possible.

This is, however, a contentious subject and at the end of the day you should, after weighing up the arguments, arrive at your own decision in a captain-like manner.

The imaginary runway

If you operate from a large airfield with long runways, you really need to impose upon yourself some habitual limitations. Using the whole length of available runway was all very well as a student, but from now on you are going to regard your personal runway as beginning (for instance) at the piano keys and ending 100m before the intersection. In other words, your imaginary runway is something between 300 and 600m long, depending on what sort of aircraft you fly and your degree of skill. Furthermore, the imaginary runway width is now only two wingspans. So touching down 5m left or right of the centreline lands you straight in the imaginary rough. Only by imposing these restrictions on yourself will you be able, in time, to acquire the judgement needed to touch down accurately every time

I suggest that you use the distance, including 30% factoring, which the POH/FM for your aircraft requires for a fully laden condition in nil wind for a landing from 50ft over the threshold. Work out how much that comes to, and then work out where your imaginary runway ends on your real-life base runways. Then find out (from a Flight Guide or the AIP) the actual runway width and reduce the imaginary width to about two wingspans. So if the actual width is say, 46m and your aircraft has a wing span of 30ft, your imaginary runway width is only two-fifths of the actual. Distribute your imaginary runway equally either side of the centre line and then you will still have plenty of asphalt "off runway" on both sides.

Strive to operate at all times within these space limitations. In time and in appropriate conditions you may be able to reduce your imaginary runway further, but this is less important than getting into the discipline of making all your final approaches so that you land accurately at the selected touch-down point at the correct speed.

Runway 26 at Exeter Airport. This has standard Precision Approach Runway markings. Conveniently the pairs of markings in the touchdown zone are at 150m intervals. This runway is 46m wide, so you ought to use less than half the width

Short-field take-offs

Practice short take-offs from your imaginary runway. Make sure that any spare actual runway is beyond rather than behind your imaginary stretch, so that in the event of a real engine failure on take-off there is a better chance of getting down again within the actual runway. Your imaginary runway for take off should include a go/no go point. This is the point, typically about 200 or 300m from the end of the imaginary runway, at which an abort can successfully be accomplished without running into the imaginary hedge at the end. All real-life short-field take-offs need such a point and it is best marked with a stick in the ground if there is no obvious alternative marker.

The clearly understood drill must be that as you come up to the marker, you ask yourself whether you will be well airborne by the end of the runway and easily able to clear any obstructions beyond the take-off run. If not, smartly close the throttle, apply brakes and abandon the take-off. Bouncing onwards beyond this point, wondering whether you will clear the hedge and whether you should abandon the attempt, is no way to go about a short-field take-off. Do remember that you can have as many abandoned attempts at take-off as you like, as long as you abandon before the go/no go marker. But you only get the one go after you have passed it. It's too late then to think about shedding weight or waiting for a better headwind or a drier surface.

The constant-attitude short-field take-off

The standard short-field take-off as usually taught in the PPL syllabus includes acceleration to the recommended rotate speed; lifting off at this speed; holding just above the ground while accelerating in ground effect until Vx (best angle-of-climb speed) is reached; climbing at this speed until 300ft AGL is reached; raising any flap; and then continuing the climb at Vy (best rate-of-climb speed).

There is another school of thought which advocates flying attitude rather than speed. The point is made that rotation speed for a light aircraft is usually a rather uncertain quantity. Some aircraft manuals quote just one speed based on maximum all-up weight. Some give a range of speeds, such as 65-75kts. However, the point to bear in mind is that the angle of attack required is a constant although rotation speed will vary with weight. The technique is simply to memorise the attitude required to maintain Vx (best angle-of-climb speed) and to adopt this attitude once the speed on your take-off run has reached somewhere around stalling speed. The aircraft will then take-off automatically as it reaches rotate speed, pause in ground effect and then climb out at Vx with no further adjustments in attitude being required. Memorising your attitude at Vx may be a small chore, but the effort will be well repaid by the ease with which you will be able to carry out optimum short-field take-offs. In point of fact, this technique is very similar to the soft-ground take-off which you will also have been taught, except that the nosewheel is raised earlier in that case.

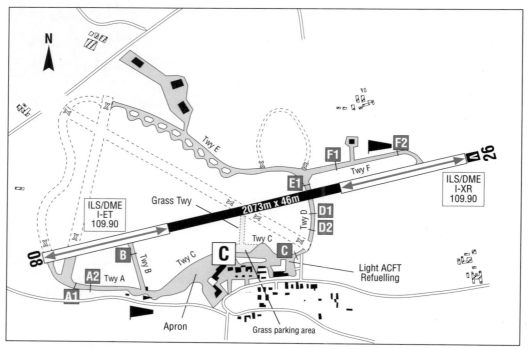

The airfield plan of Exeter Airport.
Reproduced with permission from the UK VFR Flight Guide

Imaginary 600m runway lengths are shown from the thresholds of both 08 and 26

Take-off decision point. Beyond this point you cannot safely abandon your take off

Landings

Landings

Chapter 5

Controlling Speed and Rate of Descent on the Approach

In days of yore, instructors always taught that on the approach you should control airspeed with pitch and maintain the correct glideslope with throttle. This technique soon persuaded the student to understand that on the approach, or anywhere else for that matter, throttle and pitch are interrelated. As you sailed down the glideslope in your Tiger Moth you soon appreciated that if you were, say, too low on the approach it was not a good idea merely to ease back on the stick. This was because as you reduced your rate of descent, so you inevitably decreased your speed. So now, as well as being too low, you had also become too slow – and being low and slow is just what you want to avoid. Likewise, pitching the nose down if too high on the approach without reducing throttle would inevitably lead to an increase above the desired approach speed. The increase or reduction of power would tend to make the aircraft pitch up or down in the desired direction anyway. In any case, no pilot who has sensed that he or she is low or high on the glideslope will allow the condition to continue, but will instinctively use the pitch control to adjust the rate of descent. The technique taught was (and still is) a good device for getting students to co-ordinate properly their applications of pitch and throttle.

Most small light aircraft have relatively low mass and inertia, high form drag and reasonably quick throttle response. A large jet aircraft, by comparison, displays high mass and inertia, lower form drag and a throttle response which at moments of crisis seems to take several lifetimes to spool up from low power. If you find yourself low on the glideslope when piloting a jet on the approach and you respond with the Tiger Moth pilot's technique of increasing the power, nothing much will happen for a while. This is firstly because of the slow throttle response and secondly because the great inertia causes further delay. Equally, the great inertia and lower form drag of a jet dictate that if your speed is too high it takes some time for a reduction in throttle and/or rate of descent to have much effect. So the old-fashioned technique is not appropriate for a jet, and its pilots are therefore taught to adjust speed with throttle and glideslope with pitch control. The need to co-ordinate pitch and throttle remains as before, but the cardinal requirement for the jet pilot is to monitor the speed on the approach to a degree which usually amazes piston pilots at first. You simply *have* to nail that speed and catch any departure before it has a chance to develop into anything the least bit significant. If you allow the speed to become significantly too high, you may not have time to reduce it again before the threshold and you must therefore go around. If you let it get significantly too slow, you may find yourself in a condition which is completely irrecoverable without several thousand feet of height in hand.

A jet on approach. The engines have a slow response and the aircraft has high inertia

A light aircraft on the approach. The engine responds rapidly and is easily able to overcome the relatively small inertia

Because most military and commercial pilots are eventually destined to fly jet aircraft, the old-fashioned method of controlling speed on the approach with pitch and glideslope with throttle is seldom taught today, even at basic training level. The private pilot, however, is not necessarily moving up to jets and for the PPL the technique holds as good as ever, forcing the pilot inescapably into proper co-ordination of pitch control and throttle. This is particularly desirable when you start shaving off approach speeds for short-field landings. It is absolutely vital for the aviator approaching at only a little above stalling speed to be instinctively aware of the relationship between pitch and power. If you are not thinking of becoming a jet pilot, therefore, but you are likely to be flying close to the ground and close to the stall, I commend to you the hoary and hallowed method.

The Touch-down Problem

You will no doubt have had burnt into your memory cells that a good touch-down flows from a good approach, which flows from a good base leg, which flows for all I know from good genes, a good breakfast and a good religious upbringing. However, I confess to many a less-than-good touch-down after a perfectly satisfactory approach, and it has been borne in upon me as I clunk uncomfortably on to the runway yet again that there is actually more to this business than just getting the approach right. Actually I can recall a few **good** touch-downs after **poor** approaches. Indeed, I will confess further to having been a habitually poor "toucher-down" for about the first thousand hours of my flying. I should very much like to announce that I then discovered at this point some infallible nostrum which cured all my problems and which I can now reveal to an expectant world. Alas, all I can say is that for no particular reason the touch-downs seemed to improve.

This was, of course, something of a relief because I have always been very conscious of the fact that passengers usually seem to judge the ability of their pilot from the touch-down. You may fly a faultless route in highly adverse conditions, but they ignore all that and make snide remarks about enjoying three touch-downs for the price of only one landing (or, as a passenger once said to the sub-editor of this book, "Did we land or were we shot down?").

If you do not have a particular problem with your landings, you can skip the next passage. However, if you do, come into the corner with me for an unofficial meeting of Shaky Touchers-Down Anonymous and we will see what a bit of mutual support can do. While I cannot offer a quick fix for the afflicted aviator, I can at least offer advice as to how best to live with the disease until experience brings its own cure. My advice is simply to aim for safety throughout the touch-down and never mind trying to get the wheels to kiss the runway. If they ever should do so, just regard that as one of life's little bonuses.

Concentrate therefore on these five essentials:

1   Getting the approach right. All right, I admit it – it does make life easier when you arrive at the actual moment of truth.

2   Make very sure that you arrive over the hedge at just the right speed. If the speed is too high you will float for ever, giving plenty of opportunity for much pilot-induced oscillation as your nerves get the better of you while you wait for the speed to decay. If the speed is too low you may not achieve a round-out at all and instead make a naval-style deck landing – unwise in an aircraft not designed for this activity.

3   Hold off and then hold-off some more, and don't touch down until the nose is well up in the air. This is vital to avoid the nosewheel touching down first, leading to wheelbarrowing and disaster. Furthermore, I find that holding-off until close to stalling speed brings other benefits. Your eventual touch-down will be at a lower speed, which makes for safety, and the act of progressively checking back on the pitch keeps you in control throughout and makes a gentle touch-down more likely.

4   Be ready to use throttle to check a descent from too high a hold-off, or from ballooning.

5   If you think that the landing is becoming unsafe in any way, *immediately go around.*

Contrast this with the landing technique adopted by so many. This consists of arriving at the threshold far too fast; getting the aircraft into an attitude that is vaguely hoped to be just sufficiently pitched up to keep the nosewheel from touching down first; and then simply waiting for events to unfold.

To land safely you must **fly the aircraft** all the way to the runway. Never simply sit and wait for Nature to take its course; control events yourself right up to the point at which the aircraft stops so that at least you remain master of the machine and the situation.

Crosswind Landing

The PPL syllabus covers both the crabbing and the wing-down techniques. The crabbing technique requires the pilot to apply a drift angle to the heading on final approach sufficient to counteract the crosswind and keep the aircraft on track. This exactly replicates the way you adjust your heading when flying a route so as to maintain a required track in a crosswind; the difference is that on finals you make your adjustment by eye instead of by whizzy-wheel. This method is apt to work well until touch-down, when your aircraft is still tracking the runway faultlessly but your wheels are inconveniently pointing in the direction of your heading rather than your track. To avoid wiping them off on landing, you apply rudder just before touch-down so as to align the aircraft with the runway. You have to do this before touching down but only *just* before. Too early an application of rudder will give the crosswind time to overcome your momentum down the runway and then carry you sideways across it.

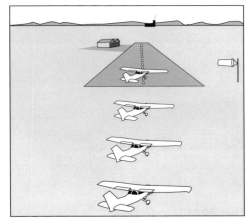

An aircraft on a crabbing approach

In the wing-down technique, you apply bank on the approach into the crosswind and – to stop the aircraft's desire to turn in the direction of the bank – you apply opposite rudder sufficient to continue down the extended runway centreline. You maintain this crossed-controls condition all the way down to touch-down, so there is no last-minute straightening up to worry about; there is just a conventional round-out, hold-off and landing. Because you carry this out with a wing down, your lower wheel will touch down before the higher one – followed by the third one in a nosewheel aircraft and also in a tailwheel aircraft if you are executing a "wheeler" landing. If you are flying a tailwheel aircraft and going for a three-pointer, your lower main and tailwheel will touch more or less simultaneously. Throughout the approach and landing you are in a sideslip, which will increase form drag. To overcome this you must either increase your power or your rate of descent.

Side slipping in on a wing down approach

You may well have been shown both techniques during your training. I was brought up on the crabbing technique and came to the wing-down method much later. While you must make up your own mind, I am bound to say that in my humble opinion the wing-down method knocks spots off the crabbing method. The main reason for this is that the wing-down technique leaves you in control of the aircraft all the way to the runway. Indeed it leaves you still flying the aircraft, if you wish, with one wheel on and the others in the air. A further benefit is that you arrive on the runway with into-wind aileron already applied, as it needs to be for the landing run in a crosswind. With the crabbing technique there comes a *moment critique* where you decide that you are about to touch down; you straighten up, and you then hope that your timing was good and you will actually touch down just as you do so. If your timing was not so good, or perhaps there comes a gust or a lull, you may find things going wrong. You are not really flying the aircraft at this point – just hoping that the thing is shortly going to cease flying – and recovering the situation if it should go wrong, may be a lot more difficult than would have been the case if you had been in control throughout the manoeuvre.

All in all, I accept that in some cases such as gliders and motor gliders the wing-down method cannot be used, but where it can be used I believe it should be.

The Imaginary Runway

The imaginary runway described in the chapter on take-offs comes into its own once more on landing. Always aim to land within it and thus learn how to fly your aircraft to (but not beyond) its limits.

The Spot Landing

If you always cross the hedge at the same speed, height, power setting and angle of descent, and if you always flare at the same height and touch-down in the same attitude, you will always land on the same spot given constant aircraft weight and configuration and constant meteorological conditions.

To achieve consistently good spot landings you therefore need to standardise your approach and landing technique, thus cutting out as many variables as possible. You need to recognize that your aiming point – which is the point at which your approach ends, the flare is commenced and the throttle closed – is some small distance from the touch-down point. So your aiming point should be an appropriate distance upwind of the desired touch-down point. All this is pretty academic stuff if you are landing a light aircraft on a 1000m runway, but once you start doing spot landings (or short-field landings for that matter) it becomes significant. Decide, therefore what is the appropriate distance required on the day in question, and move your aiming point downwind of the required "spot" accordingly.

The nearer your speed at the aiming point is to stalling speed, the shorter will be your float and the closer your aiming point to the touch-down.

The Short-field Landing

The short-field landing is all about minimum energy. Energy at the point of crossing the hedge comes from power, height and groundspeed.

Let's get power out of the way first. Once you have touched down, you don't need it. So make sure that when you close the throttle your really do *close* it. A surprising number of pilots used to endless stretches of tarmac in front of them almost close the throttle but don't quite close it fully. Those extra 200RPM above idle scarcely matter if you have 1000m of runway ahead. They may prolong your float slightly and you may take a little longer to slow to a stop, but 100m of extra float and another 100m of extra landing run will not be significant in these circumstances. Adding an extra 200m on to a short-field landing, however, may well lead to an unwelcome encounter with the far hedge – and all for such an unnecessary oversight.

As far as height is concerned, I don't personally subscribe to the short-landing technique of dragging the aircraft in on a low approach and hanging on the propeller, so that when the power is chopped just past the hedge the aircraft immediately sinks to the ground. I dislike this technique because:

1   On any but the most powerful aircraft, it is entirely possible to get so slow that you are well
      on the wrong side of the drag curve and you just don't have enough power available to
      increase speed. On a conventional approach you have the option of increasing your rate of
      descent as well as powering up so as to recover the situation. By reducing your angle of

attack you are reducing the induced drag, and at the same time Sir Isaac Newton is giving you an extra bit of thrust. (Well, all right, if you want to be pedantic, you are aligning the thrust line of the aircraft more nearly to the vertical weight line so as to derive greater benefit from the force of gravity acting upon the aircraft.) On the low-and-slow drag-in you do not have this option and risk collecting the near hedge.

2   Dragging in on a low and slow approach with the nose pitched well up makes it difficult to see ahead. This may not matter in a spot-landing competition in the middle of a large airfield. However, if you are landing in a real live short field, there may well be all sorts of hazards arranged around the touch-down point. You emphatically do not want restricted vision at this stage.

So stick to the usual approach angle. However, instead of crossing the near hedge at 50ft, aim for sufficient clearance for safety – but no more because height means energy.

The third energy constituent – groundspeed – is all-important. It is of course made up of surface wind and your airspeed. If you are in any doubt about the importance of surface wind to a short-field landing, you only have to consult your POH/FM to discover the difference a headwind of only 10kts makes to the required distance compared with the requirement in still air. Now have a look at the situation with a 10-knot tailwind…

On a fully laden PA28 Series II Arrow, for instance, the figures after factoring are 775m in a 10-knot headwind, 875m in still air and 1125m in a 10-knot tailwind. So you ignore the surface wind at your peril.

The remaining component of the groundspeed is your airspeed, and this is something entirely under your control. Taking into account your aircraft weight on the day, any gusting of the surface wind, the slope of the runway, your degree of skill and whatever the POH/FM might have to say on the subject, decide and **write down**:

■   Your stalling speed in approach configuration at today's weight.

■   Your target airspeed over the hedge.

For example, you might discover from the POH/FM (or failing that from actual experiment at a safe height) that today's stalling speed in approach configuration is 58kts. The classic approach speed is 1·3 times this, or 75kts. To this, you will recall, you should add half of any forecast gusts. So if the met man is talking about a surface wind of 15kts gusting 25, you should add a further five knots. Let's assume that today is a non-gusty day.

The short-field landing is usually carried out at a lower than normal approach speed. Subject to anything which the POH/FM may say, you must decide how much less than the 1·3 increment of stalling speed you wish to go. There is no need in the early stages of the approach to scrape along just above the stalling speed, and indeed you definitely should not normally let the speed fall below your usual approach speed until after turning final. So you will emerge from your turn on to final at 1·3Vs and allow that speed to taper off down the final approach to your target speed over the hedge.

The latter should be the POH/FM-derived short-field approach speed, if it gives one. In time, and after careful thought and discussion with pilots more experienced on your type, you may decide in certain conditions to accept a lower target speed than this. You will thereby reduce the energy present as you cross the hedge, which is a Good Thing, but on some types and in some conditions you may also be reducing significantly your degree of control and ability to recover from an incipient stall/spin. This may be confidently described as a Bad Thing.

Many light-aircraft types give you full control in the approach configuration right down to the stall, and reasonable warning of the onset of a stall or a wing drop. Others run out of full control authority as they near the stall. You need to discover, at a safe height and under suitable supervision at first, just how your usual aircraft behaves at different speeds close to the stall in different configurations and also, especially if a four-seater, at different weights. The chapter on 'Practising your Scales' gives you some help in going about this.

If the Flight Manual gives no short-field approach speed, you will have to work something out for yourself. Discuss the issue with experienced pilots on your type, practice at a safe height and then make your own mind up, as an aircraft captain should.

In the example we were working on above, the stalling speed in approach configuration was 58kts and the normal approach speed was 75kts. You might select a target speed over the hedge of 63kts. Now that's only five knots above stalling speed. The stall warning horn will be blaring away and you will be operating very close to the edge. But you will be only about ten feet above the ground, you will be monitoring the speed closely and you will be aware that you cannot make any but the most gentle turns at this speed. You will be ready to catch any wing drop with rudder and you should have just enough energy in hand to complete the round-out successfully. Even so, if you propose to operate at a speed as close to the stall as this, you *must* be in good practice and familiar with both the aircraft and the landing ground. In the same example a pilot with less skill and/or experience might select a target speed over the hedge of 68kts. The margin of ten knots above the stalling speed gives the pilot more time and energy to correct any difficulties which may arise. But it also gives more energy to dissipate in the float and the landing run.

Forced Landings

Forced Landings

One of the more formidable ingredients of the Skill Test for the PPL (and, indeed, for the CPL) is the Practice Forced Landing. There is always some concern on the part of the candidate as to whether this part of the test is going to conclude with the aircraft nicely lined up for a glide approach comfortably positioned for an upwind landing one-third of the way into a large level well-drained and unobstructed field with a suitable surface for an uneventful arrival. In a real-life forced landing, such a happy conclusion is alas all too rare. And even when it has been achieved, it seems that there can still be a sting in the tail. One of the few pilots I know who actually found such a field and landed in it was so delighted with his prowess and his general good fortune that he dealt with his minor engine problem, restarted it and then attempted a take-off which ended in the far hedge…

From this unfortunate tale we learn two universal truths about flying, viz.:

1   What might do in emergency needs to be considered again *de novo* when you have the luxury of choice.
2   Most light aircraft need a longer take-off distance than they do a landing distance.

Your Imaginary Runway

A passage in the chapter on take-offs describes how you need to limit your operations on a large runway to an imaginary area which is somewhat smaller. In this way you will acquire the habit of being parsimonious with runway lengths and widths. Only by acquiring such habits of judgement when carrying out conventional landings will you be able to increase significantly your chance of pulling off a successful forced landing if you should ever encounter the Awful Silence.

Practice Forced Landings

Having persuaded yourself always to land within your imaginary runway, the next challenge is to do it from a glide approach. To start with, you can perform Practice Forced Landings (PFLs) from overhead the airfield. However, establishments with large hard-surfaced runways are often not particularly keen on light aircraft repeatedly carrying out PFLs. This is because they like to keep their magnificent stretches of asphalt ready at all times to receive the far more remunerative wheels of commercial traffic. However, the antipathy of such places towards a private pilot wishing to carry out a PFL can often turn out to be somewhat less than you might imagine from conversation around the local flying-club bar. The secret is to phone up ATC and discuss the possibilities. Many regional airports have times when traffic is slack and can easily fit in a prearranged PFL. On the other hand, the pilot who calls on the radio requesting an immediate PFL on an *ad hoc* basis is much more likely to be refused, even if there are apparently very few movements at the time. Learn to negotiate with ATC, and also learn that this is much more easily done over the phone than it is over the radio.

The full-scale PFL from 3000ft or so down to the airfield is as much a practice of the initial approach procedure – arriving in good order at the chosen 1000ft (or 1500ft if you prefer) mark – as it is of the final approach and touch-down. In my view, the initial approach procedure is probably better practised away from the airfield, with a field selected in the heat of your simulated emergency as the predicated landing point, than it is from overhead the airfield. After all, the chances of a real engine failure happening to occur at 3000ft over your airfield are unfortunately rather rare, and the PFL from overhead the airfield as taught to student PPLs is only an introduction to the subject.

The final approach and touch-down part of a PFL can be practised as part of ordinary landings as discussed below. However, selection of a suitable field, planning the approach strategy and selecting the defined approach points and heights are best performed in the far more realistic conditions away from the airfield.

If flying on a mutual basis, you may agree between yourselves before take-off that the non-handling pilot may impose an imaginary engine problem at any time (subject to the arrangements suggested in the passage on mutual flying in chapter 2) so as to give the handling pilot some more realistic practice

So head out into the open country to practise selecting the best field available, identifying the desired downwind position and height (or High and Low Key positions) and then manoeuvering yourself to your positions in good order with all checks completed. Remember the "S Code" when selecting your field:

> Shape – Slope – Size – Surface – Surroundings

and try to find an opportunity subsequently to inspect from the ground your chosen fields to see how they compare with how they seemed from the air.

Whatever method you use for the last couple of thousand feet or so of your forced landing, it will probably involve getting yourself to a predetermined point at a predetermined height AGL and conducting your standard approach to the selected field from there. And here we meet what is probably the most serious area of difficulty for the pilot out of practice in forced landings. This is judgement of the gliding angle of the aircraft once the engine has stopped. Most out-of-practice pilots have a very optimistic idea of the gliding characteristics of their aircraft. Reading the accident statistics reveals that forced landings often end up with touchdowns in places other than the pilot can have originally intended; trees, high standing crops and so on. We are not usually told exactly how this came about, but in most cases it will be because the pilot failed to make it to the selected field. Either the touch-down was then made in the undershoot area or the aircraft ended in worse trouble as a result of trying to stretch the glide.

Glide Angle

It is well worth while investigating the gliding characteristics of your particular aircraft type. From the manual you can discover the best glide speed and possibly the rate of descent at this speed. If no rate of descent is quoted, you can easily establish it with a stopwatch during a glide through a couple of thousand feet or so.

An important point to appreciate at this juncture is that the rate of descent of an aircraft with its engine ticking over and its propeller windmilling is less than it will be with the engine (and propeller) fully stopped. While you practice your forced landings and carry out your glide approaches with the engine ticking over, if the big day ever comes the engine is likely to be completely stopped. The difference may contribute to the poor forced landing results these days. To allow for the difference I suggest that you add an extra one or two hundred feet per minute to your rate of descent with the engine ticking over during forced landing and glide approach practice. Alternatively, take along your favourite instructor one day and, with the co-operation of ATC and overhead an airfield with a long runway, shut down the engine at a good height –

The glide angle mark on a high wing aircraft

say 6000ft. You can then investigate the glide characteristics with the engine off: on some aircraft this is markedly different to the rate of descent achieved with idle power. Restart the engine in good time and until you have done so conduct the flight on the basis that the engine is not going to oblige and you are going to have to perform a 'dead stick' landing for real. Power pilots may find this proposition alarming but glider and motor glider pilots will wonder what all the fuss is about.

Having determined your rate of descent at best glide speed, you need to discover the gliding *angle*. This is an extremely useful piece of information to a pilot in charge of a former powered aircraft which has suddenly become a glider. It tells you the angle at which you are going to be going down, and hence which bits of the ground beneath you are going to be within gliding distance and which are not. By the use of the rate-of-descent figures and the best glide speed, it becomes a matter of simple trigonometry to calculate the glide angle. However, for the sake of those for whom a few minutes with calculator and trigonometry tables would be wearisome, I bring you, at absolutely no extra charge, the following:

Glide-angle Ready Reckoner

BEST GLIDE SPEED – KNOTS

ROD						
FPM	**50**	**60**	**70**	**80**	**90**	**100**
500	6°	5°	4°	4°	3°	3°
600	7°	6°	5°	4°	4°	3°
700	8°	7°	6°	5°	4°	4°
800	9°	7°	6°	6°	5°	5°
900	10°	8°	7°	6°	6°	5°
1000	11°	9°	8°	7°	6°	6°
1100	13°	10°	9°	8°	7°	7°
1200	14°	12°	10°	9°	8°	7°

From this table you should be able to discover the glide angle of any conventional light aircraft.

"But what", I hear you ask, "is the use of that piece of information?"

The glide angle mark on a low wing aircraft

"With a protractor held to your eye", I reply, "you can sit in your particular aircraft and see the actual glide angle."

"Do you seriously expect me to get out a protractor when the engine fails and set about calculating where the whole unpleasant experience is going to end?" you exclaim.

"No, of course not tiresome reader" I reply. In fact, what you do is to look along your protractor just once, when the aircraft is safely parked, and then look out sideways. If yours is a low-wing aircraft, note what point on the leading edge is intersected by the glide angle from your eye. It might, for instance, be two feet in from the tip, or perhaps one foot beyond the tip. If you have a high-wing aircraft you will probably do well to find a point in relation to the strut.

As a further guide, turn the protractor upside-down and note how far beneath the horizon your particular glide angle cuts. You can use this version of the glide-angle guide even when your aircraft is banked.

You may now dispense with the protractor for good and all as far as forced landings are concerned. From now on, you have only to look out and know that everything on the ground within the circle whose centre is immediately beneath you – and whose circumference passes through that point on the ground in line with your reference point (or those points if you are using the angle beneath the horizon as your guide) – is within gliding distance. Naturally this technique assumes still air and will have to be adjusted for wind effect, but it is nonetheless an extremely useful guide and should be used at all times during a forced landing. This means that as your height AGL decreases, you have a constant guide as to what is within gliding distance. Remember never to let your chosen field stray towards the edge of your range at any given height and you will have overcome the most common cause of forced-landing failure.

Glide Approaches

It has to be said that the accident statistics show a rather depressing incidence of failure in judging forced landings, so that engine failures tend to end in damage to the aircraft and sometimes injury to the occupants. The received wisdom is that this is caused by a lack of practice on the part of PPLs. There seems to be not much doubt that forced landings met with more success in the 1920s and 1930s than they do today, and this is assuredly because in those days glide approaches were the rule rather than the exception

In still air, anything which lies within the circumference passing through the Glide Angle mark is within gliding range

which they are nowadays. In the pre-war RAF, indeed, a powered approach witnessed by assembled officers required the subsequent purchase of a round of drinks in the Mess. Furthermore, the poorer reliability of pre-war engines no doubt made keeping in practice at forced landings much more pressing than it is seen to be today.

A pilot whose approaches are usually glide approaches is naturally going to be in better practice for judging a forced landing than is a pilot who habitually makes powered approaches. Apart possibly from engine cooling requirements, there is no reason why every approach to land at an airfield which you make should not be a glide approach and thus a practice for a forced-landing final approach and touch-down. So my suggestion is that a good proportion of your everyday landings should be carried out as glide approaches. Maintain normal circuit height with flaps up on the base leg until you judge that you can comfortably glide to a touchdown one-third into your (maybe imaginary) runway. Throttle back to idle (carb heat out, remember; you just might need that engine again in a minute or so) and carry out a glide approach. If you are forced to fly wide circuits and/or there is a strong headwind component on finals, you may even find yourself leaving the circuit power on and maintaining circuit height until somewhere on finals. You will quickly learn that reducing the power too early leaves you with few possible measures for recovering the position. You can try cutting the corner from crosswind to finals if you are flying a conventional forced landing, and tightening the turn should be a remedy if you are flying the constant-aspect method. But these measures may not be sufficient to avoid landing in the undershoot, and eventually you have to apply power again. Then you may feel glad that at least you remembered to pull the carb heat so as to give you a nicely de-iced and responsive engine when you want it.

Cutting the power too late, however, leaves you with rather more options. Applying flap (check the speed is within the flap lowering limit) is the obvious remedy, but it may not be enough. If by now you have mastered the aircraft handling section of this book, are competent and practised in sideslipping and the POH/FM allows it, you can lose excess height in that way. You can try diving off the excess height, although this is of only limited value on many aircraft. Alternatively you can S-turn or dog-leg the approach.

But remember – do not exceed 45° angle of bank at any time.

Yes, I know that you are a pilot of outstanding ability and that 45° is a puny angle of bank for such an ace as yourself. However, reflect that loss of control is the most common cause of fatalities in light aircraft, and that there is not likely to be sufficient height to recover from an inadvertent stall or spin. In concentrating so hard on getting this tortuous approach right, you are a perfect candidate for admission to the lists of those unfortunates who, when close to the ground, allowed the angle-of-attack and airspeed combination to exceed the limit for controlled flight.

Reflect further that even at a miserable 45° angle of bank, the stalling speed will be around 20% higher than the wings-level value. It's all too easy for 45° to creep up inadvertently to 60°, when the stalling speed will become over 40% more – and that has now exceeded the conventional approach speed of $1.3V_s$. So keep the speed well up during such manoeuvres, especially when so close to the ground, and *watch that angle of bank.*

The Low and Slow Turn

Remember also the extra perils of the turn from downwind to upwind at low speed and low level. This has caught many an unfortunate pilot out, and is one of the "gotchas" facing those who fly low and slow. There are armchair experts who will tell you that your aircraft neither knows nor cares whether you are flying downwind or upwind – it flies through the air just the same, and is carried where the wind listeth all unknowing. The said "experts" are undoubtedly right so far as aerial navigation is concerned, but dangerously wrong when it comes to aircraft banking close to the ground. If you have been practising your scales (see chapter 3) the low-flying exercise will have awoken you to the danger here. When you come fairly close to the ground, it becomes instinctive to judge your speed by the rate the ground beneath you passes by. In effect you are inclined to think groundspeed rather than airspeed, and in high winds that is a dangerous and misleading practice. So the specific lesson to be learned from all this is that when flying close to the ground in high winds, you have to be on your guard to watch the ASI continually and not judge your airspeed from your passage over the ground.

It may well be that in your early attempts, you find that you cannot lose sufficient height within the limitation of 45° maximum Angle Of Bank. If so, resist the temptation to increase the angle of bank and instead just throw the approach away. If you are trying to land within an imaginary area forming part of a larger runway, you may be able to complete your landing within the full runway. However, if there is any doubt at all about there being sufficient runway, go around and have another try. It's all good experience and part of the business of improving your flying skills step by step. Of course, if you had gone for a normal powered approach you would have carried out a normal and safe landing with no need to call attention to yourself by having to go around. But if you never push yourself just a little beyond your present skill level (always leaving yourself a safe means of recovery if necessary) you will never improve.

More about Glide Approaches

Making glide approaches and judging the correct point at which to close the throttle will soon bring an important point home to you. This is the very considerable effect the degree of headwind has on your approach when there is no engine to overcome the wind's effect. Indeed, gliders flown in high winds sometimes have to aim for a position vertically over the threshold because their approach speed may equal the windspeed aloft.

As you continue to practice, you will soon come to ask yourself habitually as you plan any glide approach, "What is the wind strength and direction today?" and to make the appropriate allowance for you particular aircraft. If you find yourself one day in a real forced-landing situation, you will *instinctively* ask yourself this vital question.

If you are flying a retractable, you will no doubt have a strategy of leaving your wheels up until you are quite confident of being able to reach the desired touch-down point. When practising, however, this procedure has two disadvantages. The first is the insistent warning horn which starts as soon as you throttle

Always know what the wind is doing. Nothing at all on this occasion, which will mean long glides and ground runs

back and continues until the wheels are down and locked. The second is that if you leave lowering the undercarriage until the last 100ft so as to maximise your glide performance, you are risking forgetting it altogether. I therefore recommend carrying out your practice glide approaches with wheels down all the way. Admittedly this will give you more drag – but if you ever find yourself carrying out a forced landing for real, you will discover that the windmilling propeller gives you far more drag than you ever experienced with the engine at idle. So to a degree, the extended undercarriage will simulate the drag of a windmilling propeller.

In a real-life forced landing you will leave your retractable undercarriage raised until you are sure of making it into the field. You will need to leave the battery master switch on if the wheels are lowered electrically and one of the advantages of having a truly dead engine is that you can now advance the throttle so as to kill the undercarriage warning horn if you dislike the racket at such a trying time.

If you have a variable-pitch propeller, you should set the pitch to fully coarse in an actual engine failure because this will reduce the drag of the windmilling blades. Do not on any account, however, select coarse pitch during a practice forced landing; just carry out a touch drill instead. If you were to select coarse pitch during a practice and you then had to go around – and you forgot to select fine pitch before opening the throttle – you could easily find that your practice engine failure had become a real one in no time at all. And just when you discovered that you really needed that engine after all...

Forced Landings – Two Schools of Thought

There are two schools of thoughts as to how best to conduct the approach for a forced landing. The traditional school advocates aiming to arrive at the beginning of the downwind leg of a conventional square circuit at about 2000ft AGL, turning in for the base leg when you are abeam or just past the aiming point (which is usually one-third into your field) and probably reaching a point about 1000ft AGL somewhere on the base leg. This leg should be closer to the aiming point than your base leg would be to the threshold on a conventional powered circuit. This then gives you the opportunity to adjust your approach by turning away somewhat from the field and/or extending the leg. On the other hand, if you find yourself running out of height you can cut into the field. The most common mistakes made are firstly to overestimate the gliding capacity of the aircraft with engine off and secondly to fly the downwind leg too close to the field and to extend it too far beyond abeam the aiming point. This usually results in the pilot having to make a steep and almost 180° turn followed by a straight-in approach, thus losing the valuable opportunity for height adjustment in the turn on to finals.

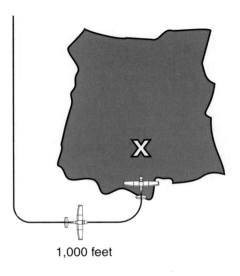

1,000 feet

The Traditional Forced Landing

Constant-aspect Approaches

A very useful alternative to the traditional version of the forced landing is the 'constant aspect' approach. Still regarded by some instructors as a dangerous departure from the true religion, it was in fact adopted by the RAF as long ago as the 1970s, having been for even longer the approved procedure of the RCAF. Its proponents claim that here is a method which is far more likely to end in a successfully judged approach, and because it calls for less judgement it needs less practice and experience than does the traditional method. Its detractors object that it is inappropriate for high-wing aircraft, and that for all users there is a risk of the method ending in a screaming spiral dive into the ground.

All this is wonderfully controversial stuff for arguments around the flying-club bar, but at the end of the day it is difficult to ignore the claims made by such an august body as the RAF Central Flying School. I would strongly suggest that every serious pilot should at least learn the technique and then decide whether to adopt it in preference to the traditional method.

The constant-aspect approach is really an extension of the thinking which brought you the assessment of glide angle described above, and the rule not to let your field out of glide-angle range at any time. You should proceed as follows:

Having identified your field and your aiming point (AP) within it, set yourself up so that you are gliding down the dead side in the chosen landing direction and abeam the AP. Your height should be about 2500ft AGL, give or take about 500ft; the exact figure is not critical at this point because the method automatically adjusts for height in its execution. When the AP lies somewhere between the leading and the trailing edge in a low-wing aircraft (or in a high-wing aircraft, the AP is between the nine o'clock and the eight o'clock position – three and four o'clock in a right-hand circuit) you are at 'High Key'. You now turn crosswind and allow for drift so that you track at right angles to the landing direction.

When the AP is 45° astern, start a turn-in aiming for a constant angle of bank which should work out in the region of 20°. When you arrive abeam the AP in the downwind direction, you are in the 'Low Key' position. You then increase the angle of bank depending on the strength of the wind and your aircraft's gliding characteristics. The theory is that the tighter the turn, the less height you are going to need to complete the final 180° and arrive at the AP at ground level. You may still be turning as you cross the field boundary but you should be well set up for a touch-down at the desired AP. Your track down to the AP will be a spiral, the decrease in height at any time being matched by a reduction in the radius of your turn so as to keep the AP always within your glide angle. There will be a simultaneous decrease in the difference between your heading and the desired landing direction.

In a well executed constant-aspect approach, from 'Low Key' onwards until you straighten up for touchdown, the AP will constantly present the same aspect. In other words, the angle seen from the cockpit subtended by the horizon and the AP will remain the same. If it becomes less, you are getting too far from the AP – so you should increase your angle of bank. If it is increasing, you are getting too near and should decrease the angle of bank.

It is claimed for this method that it works for any aircraft, even if the pilot does not actually know the gliding characteristics of the machine at the time. If you have not the height to carry out the complete procedure, you can join the constant-aspect approach at some appropriate point nearer the ground.

Ask an instructor familiar with the constant-aspect approach method to show you how and then go off and practice it. But if you ever find yourself having to increase the angle of bank more than 45°, go around.

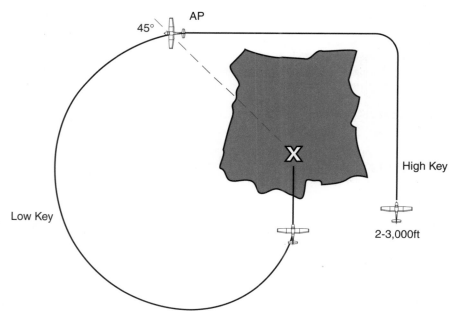

The Constant Aspect Forced Landing

How Low Should I Go?

A curious and unfortunate misunderstanding seems to have sprung up regarding practice forced landings which are continued below 500ft away from an airfield. Those who misunderstand warn of the risk of prosecution by the CAA if practices are taken down below this height. Some go on to blame the present poor success rate in actual forced landings on a punctilious and severe bureaucracy ever keen to drag innocent pilots into the dock. The misapprehenders base their dire prognostications on an alleged draconian enforcement of that part of Rule 5 of the Rules of the Air which says:

An aircraft must not fly closer than 500ft to any person, vessel, vehicle or structure.

Note, however, that this is not a height limitation and you may descend below 500ft provided that your flight path will not take you within 500ft (167 yards or 152 metres) vertically, horizontally or diagonally of any person, vessel, vehicle or structure. So in the case of a practice forced landing you may, if you are quite sure of compliance with Rule 5, carry on down to perhaps 200ft AGL. From this height you will be in no doubt whether you were going to make it at the appropriate speed to the aiming point. Indeed, you should have no difficulty in deciding at 500ft AGL whether or not this one is a winner once you become practised and adept at glide approaches

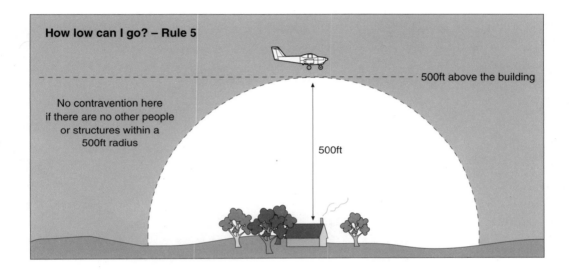

Quite apart from the law's demands, never forget that a low-flying light aircraft can often be a source of annoyance to those below – and sometimes worse in the case of sensitive livestock. So fly at all times with proper consideration. Never carry out repeated PFLs over the same area, and do choose another flight path or another practice field if your climb-away is going to take you over a farm or private houses below about 1000ft AGL. Remember another of the provisions of Rule 5 which requires a height of more than 1500ft over a 'settlement'. The interpretation of this word by the CAA is quite broad, and anything more than three or four houses might be seen by them as being within the meaning of the Rule.

Simulated Engine Failures While Mutual Flying

While you were doing your training, your instructor may well have throttled back the engine from time to time and simulated an engine failure so that you had to carry out a PFL. Mutual flying also gives a good opportunity for surprise simulations. The basis on which this might be done between consenting adults is set out in the passage about mutual flying in chapter 2. As regards simulated engine failures, I would suggest that something a bit more sophisticated than mere closing of the throttle might usefully be introduced at times. While the sudden and total stopping of the engine is good for drama and adrenalin, there are just as many instances in real life where the engine takes sick but does not necessarily expire there and then. So instead of just closing the throttle, the non-handling pilot might instead put an imaginary engine-malfunction scenario to the handling pilot and ask what action seems appropriate. Having some sensible ideas about what to do in the case of one or another sort of engine sickness calls for some understanding of the various types of engine trouble, their symptoms and the appropriate actions to take. Having such an understanding is, of course, one of the things which distinguishes the good pilot from the merely adequate.

Farm Strips

Farm Strips

Chapter 7

Private Flying's Underworld

While you will have done your training from a licensed airfield, probably with some sort of air traffic control or at least an information service, you may have become aware of a sort of underworld of flying where pilots operate from private landing strips. You may have noticed within your local area the odd private strip tucked away amongst some farmland somewhere, and you may have envied the lucky owner. Picture the scene. After a hard day of muck-spreading, Farmer Giles lays aside his smock, his bailer-twined cord trousers and his wellies; pulls the old J3 Cub out from the back of the implement shed; makes sure that the sheep are out of the North Pasture; and lifts into the calm evening air for a gentle float-around above the adjoining parishes. He has no need of radio, there is no other traffic, he has no landing fees to pay and not a care in the world.

If you want to become part of this other world of private aviation, your first stop should be the Popular Flying Association (see the Appendix) and the next stop should be the local 'strut' of that association. Here you will meet a collection of enthusiasts, many of whom operate from private strips. Not many are farmers but most are tenants of farmers, paying a good deal less for the use of the strip than they would have to pay at a licensed airfield. In addition to renting out their strip, many owners allow flying visitors by prior arrangement and you will find details of many such strips in most flight guides.

Flying from private strips is a very different world from flying from a licensed airfield. It is usually cheaper, it is far less controlled and it has about it a much greater feeling of freedom. However, with more freedom comes more responsibility. The world of club flying from licensed airfields has a large body of controls and restrictions designed to prevent pilots from bad decisions and errors of judgement. Strip flying has none of these and the pilot has to contribute a much-heightened awareness of the possible dangers and a much higher degree of self-discipline if the operations are to go ahead in a reasonably low-risk environment. This is particularly so as regards the pilot unused to strip flying, because the culture is so very different from that of the licensed airfield and club flying. Suddenly you are very much on your own – often literally – and you must learn to look for the pitfalls which never even existed before.

Freedom and Responsibility

An airfield needs to be licensed by the CAA if it is to be used for flying training or public-transport operations, but outside these activities there is no requirement for a licensed airfield. Indeed the only requirement which exists for a private pilot to land anywhere is that the landowner's consent should have been given. While you should of course check in each individual case, most aircraft insurance policies are not restricted to operations from a licensed airfield. So, having obtained the landowner's consent, it is entirely up to you as captain whether or not you deem a field suitable for your proposed operation. It is also up to you to decide whether you have the skill and the right sort of aircraft to operate safely.

Now this is a very privileged position to be in, and many Continentals would give their eye-teeth for such latitude. With the privilege, however, comes the aforesaid responsibility. If you have never flown from a private strip before, you have never had to ask yourself (apart perhaps from the issue of runway length) whether a runway is safe for your take-off and/or landing. If you start private-strip operating, however, this becomes a crucial issue to be considered before each departure or arrival. Licensed airfields have extensive protected areas around their environs so that you may assume without inquiry that nothing is likely to obstruct a normal approach, landing, take-off or go-around. Apart from physical obstructions, the possibility of disturbed wind patterns from buildings and the like around the landing and take-off areas will have been considered. Gradients will have been measured and reported. In deciding the runway lengths available, the assumption will have been made that the aircraft will be crossing the airfield boundary at 50ft above any obstruction, and the take-off distance available will similarly assume that the take-off run will have to finish in time for the aircraft to climb to 50ft above any obstruction at the far end.

It follows that the private-strip owner who tells you that his strip is 600m long is probably talking about a different sort of 600m than the 600m of TORA ('Take Off Run Available') at a licensed airfield. At the private strip there is liable to be at least a hedge or fence at the immediate end of the 600m and maybe something even more solid. At the licensed airfield there is enough space beyond the end of the 600m to allow an aircraft to climb to 50ft above the boundary hedge. These two supposedly equivalent lengths are thus very different.

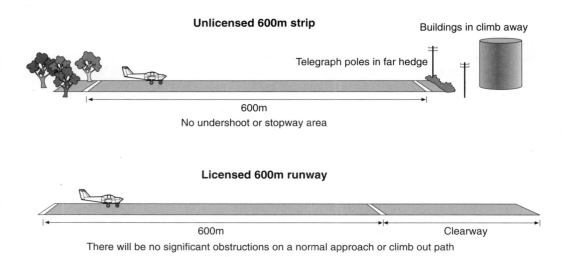

Some of the potential hazards of a 600m unlicensed strip compared with a licensed 600m runway

Be Aware

So you need to be fully aware of all the physical factors of the strip: its dimensions, gradient, surface, wind conditions, hazards on the approach and the climb-out, possible wind eddies or wind shear, areas not to be overflown and so on. As in a forced landing you need to apply the standard considerations of shape, slope, size, surface and surroundings.

You need to be aware of how your aircraft handles in short-field conditions. You need to have made the appropriate calculations of required landing and take-off distances from the POH/FM and you need to be in good practice at short-field take-offs and landings in the aircraft you will be flying from the strip – and at the same loading. It would, for instance, be foolish to fly into a strange strip in a four-seater with all seats occupied if all your short-field practice had been with only one or two up.

The more time and effort put into prior reconnaissance, the safer you should be. If you are flying to a strange strip, see if you can do so in the company of someone who is already familiar with that strip. Failing that, a prior visit by road would be valuable. You must make it an invariable practice to phone the owner as close as is convenient to your proposed time of arrival. Apart from the essential permission to use the strip, you will need any useful and timely information from the owner about the state of play at the strip at that time. There are also likely to be various areas to avoid overflying, some of which will be mentioned in the flight guide while others may not. Finding a strange strip from the air can sometimes prove very difficult. Ask for advice from the owner, or others familiar, but even then they may be so habituated to the place that they find it without conscious effort and cannot give any useful guidance as to what to look for. You sometimes receive rather hazy advice such as "Turn on to finals where the three pine trees used to be", which may not be a model of clarity.

A farm strip from downwind for 29

Left Base for the same strip. Is there much of a slope?

The steep upslope at the threshold to 29. You need to know how to land on steep slopes to land here. In a strong wind down the strip watch out for curlover on the approach

GPS can be useful but beware of differences between published co-ordinates and actual co-ordinates on the WGS84 projection which your GPS uses. GPS will certainly get you to the vicinity of the strip but may not guide you to the precise overhead. Even if you are in the vicinity, some strips are still astonishingly difficult to identify – especially if there is no aircraft on the ground at the time, no obvious hangar and nothing more reliable than a small windsock to distinguish the strip from surrounding fields. To avoid annoying the neighbours and/or unintentionally crashing the circuit, remain if you can at more than 2000ft AGL until you have positively identified the strip and planned your circuit.

Make sure that you have a definite indication of the wind conditions before starting your circuit and plan accordingly. Apart from the indications of any windsock on the field, smoke is usually the best wind indicator. The movement of cloud shadows across the fields can be useful but remember that this shows the wind at cloud height, not at ground level. A radio call to a nearby airfield will give you their wind conditions. Think about possible disturbances to the wind at ground level, especially around the threshold. Resist the temptation to fly the downwind and base legs too close to the field. Because the strip will be a good deal smaller than a conventional airfield, the scale effect will lure you much closer in than you should be. The result will inevitably be a cramped and hurried circuit followed by an arrival too high and too fast – just what you *don't* want on a short-field landing. So be mentally prepared to throw the landing away from the approach if you do not look likely to cross the hedge at the right speed and height, or if this will be achieved only by extreme manoeuvres close to the ground.

The Trickiest Bit

Having touched down in good order, do not let your concentration lapse. Your landing run is probably on a narrow runway with little stopping distance to spare, maybe with a cross gradient and often with a much poorer surface than you are used to. So keep the aircraft straight and bring it to a full stop as soon as the conditions will allow. Turn left initially after you have stopped even if right is where you need to go, so that any aircraft landing behind can overtake you on your right. Taxi with great caution; dropping a wheel into a rabbit hole or something similar could damage your propeller. If in any doubt, get a passenger to get out and clear your taxiway for you. Most landing strips have at least a signing-in book. Some have a hut or caravan where sometimes you can brew a hot drink. Some have strange people lurking in dark corners of hangars and barns working on rare and fascinating aircraft. Their initial reticence on meeting a stranger at this lonely workplace will soon give way to a torrent of information about their obsession if you seem to share it at all. I have spent many an unexpected happy hour or three in the company of such people and the unofficial light-aircraft museums of which they have the care.

"Taxi with great caution."

A sudden change in surface can mean prop strike or a damaged wheel fairing

Always discuss your departure with the owner or any other pilot on the strip. Useful information known only to the natives can often be gleaned in this manner. Unless you have the owner's permission, do not fly circuits – and even if you are positively invited to do so, on no account fly a 'beat up' of the strip. Make your departure as quiet and unobtrusive as possible. Many strip owners have ongoing problems in keeping the peace with their neighbours, who get tired of and maybe oversensitive to aircraft frequently flying low overhead. The last thing you as a guest of the owner should do is make life more difficult for them.

Any advice about farm-strip flying inevitably becomes a litany of do's and dont's which makes the whole business sound risky and uncertain. It is admittedly more risky than using a licensed airfield but not especially so provided that the pilot is aware of the pitfalls and exercises sound judgement. However, I would not be doing justice to this sort of flying if I did not also explain that every visit to a strip is a rather special adventure. I know of few more rewarding ways to spend some free time than to seek out a strip, sideslip over the hedge, trundle to a well-controlled halt and park up next to a hangar hiding some interesting aircraft. You can then consort with the denizens within, go for a country stroll (with lunch or tea maybe) and then, without having to queue up endlessly for take-off, slip quietly home again at the end of a perfect day. You will hear frustrated pilots banging endlessly on about how flying is not what it was and just no fun any more, but down in that beguiling underworld of strip flying there are pilots having just as much fun as any pilot ever did. And at very modest cost too.

It's a great shame that the average flying instructor knows very little about this sort of flying and is therefore disinclined to recommend it.

On the other hand very good advice and training on farm strip operation and other aspects of flying simple aircraft is available under the Popular Flying Association (PFA) coaching scheme. Pilots who are very experienced in this sort of flying help less experienced pilots improve their skills and develop their ability in a controlled and informed fashion. If you are new to this sort of flying the PFA coaching scheme is difficult to beat as an introduction and the costs are modest. Contact details for the PFA appear at the end of this book.

Going Places

Going Places

Chapter 8

What Have You Got it For?

If "it" is your PPL, the proper answers in most cases are:

- Getting from A to B, or
- Practising to get from A to B.

It is an unfortunate fact that student pilots are given little idea of this essential truth by their flying schools: the gaining of the qualification is seen as the whole point of the training, whereas it is really nothing of the sort. So repeat after me, and repeat it again five times every night before bedtime:

"I got my PPL so as to get around."

Of course, for wannabee commercial pilots the PPL is but a first step up a long ladder. And for just a few private pilots, the PPL is a step towards aerobatics, formation flying or some other recreational aviation mostly involving advanced handling techniques. For the vast majority of private aviators, however, the PPL is the key which unlocks the door to the challenge, the thrill, the excitement and the satisfaction of making aerial voyages – and voyages, by definition, have to start at one place and finish at another. The aerial voyage has three special advantages. First of all, it gets you very quickly and easily to a whole variety of destinations. Secondly, it gives everyone on board a special and spectacular view of the countryside passing beneath. Thirdly, it gives the crew of the aircraft a well-earned feeling of achievement at having made the voyage.

What have you got it for?

You may quite reasonably ask where these voyages should go. That will be partly a question of personal preference, but most pilots start out with day trips to other airfields – often where there is a fly-in taking place, an air show, a rally or some similar draw. Trips of this nature can make a thoroughly satisfying day out, and time spent perusing the calendar or diary sections of the flying magazines will reveal a wide variety of interesting goings-on. Beginners are always welcome at these functions, so you need have no fear of being looked down upon. The really serious and professional-looking pilots often turn out to be no more than 200-hour *poseurs* in any case. What is always important is that you obtain full details of the regulations and procedures for arrival and departure on the day from the organisers, and that you carefully adhere to them. So get a plane-full together and go off and enjoy.

Later on you may start thinking of aeronautical holidays, either in the UK or abroad. The world has become your oyster. If you cannot get your hands on an aeroplane at modest cost for a few days holiday, think about extending your experience by staying for a few days at somewhere like the Tiger Club in Kent where you can fly Jodels, Tiger Moths and Stampes. Or how about a gliding holiday, or microlighting, or a seaplane licence? One of my best holidays ever was spent by getting a cheap package flight to Florida, checking out on a PA28 Archer there and renting it at about $60 per hour so that four of us could enjoy a superb few days flying around the Bahamas from one coral-island paradise to the next. We could have spent more on a holiday in a two-star hotel in Blackpool.

The culture of most flying schools is virtually blind to the enjoyment to be had from going places. Equally, the training provided is insufficient to equip the newly qualified PPL to set out with confidence on almost any flight which extends beyond the local area. I have no particular quarrel with the contents of the PPL syllabus, nor with the training exercises. I appreciate that in fifty hours or less of basic training they have to concentrate on the basics, particularly pure aircraft handling, so as to ensure that they turn out pilots who are safe at the controls. In such a short time there is insufficient time to give a student much actual practice in route flying; in fact the dreaded qualifying cross-country is almost the only significant solo route-flying experience which most students encounter. Naturally this is a seminal event for the student. For the first time ever, they set out on a voyage into the unknown, entirely alone and with no instructor to turn to when doubts arise – as they surely will. Of course, the instructors mother the student to a considerable degree: the nav plot has to be checked, the flight authorised by a senior instructor and the destination airfields are warned of the imminent arrival of the beginer.

All this is first-class training but there is simply nowhere near enough of it. If there were five solo navexes with the degree of mothering tapering off, the schools would turn out PPL holders not only able enough but, more important, confident enough to undertake simple solo route flying without supervision. As it is, the recently qualified PPL is usually too scared to undertake another navex after qualifying and is all too likely to stick to what he or she is confident in doing. This usually amounts to flying around the good old local training area and perhaps making an occasional expedition down a well-worn route to some well-known nearby airfield for a cup of coffee.

It's small wonder really that so many recently qualified PPLs give up flying within a year or two. Wandering around the training area like a lost soul soon loses its appeal, and the more the time goes by the more forbidding becomes the prospect of flights to strange places.

My recommendation to the newly qualified PPL is to accept that the licence is no more than a licence to learn, and to accept also that the basic training was insufficient to equip a raw PPL to do what most private pilots do for enjoyment – which is to undertake aerial voyages. Therefore more skills and confidence have to be acquired so as to benefit properly from the award of the licence. Yes, I know they didn't tell you anything about this at your flying school, and perhaps you thought that getting your PPL was the very summit of your ambitions and definitely the end of having to learn. But pause and consider your brilliant career as a cyclist. At first your mentor had to run along behind you holding the saddle. Then one magical day you wobbled down the lawn unaided; your first solo! Soon you were careering all over the place and your parents were setting limits to your radius of operation. After a while the magic of pure bicycle handling – swooping around bends, dodging around the flower beds and staying out of the fish pond – began to pall and by degrees the bike became a vehicle rather than a toy. The old thrills of pure handling would still return as you cycled from here to there, and in addition there was the satisfaction and the independence of having your own wheels which would take you wherever you chose.

So it is with flying. As a newly fledged PPL you are now allowed out of the garden and down to the end of the road, but if you never go past the front gate you will never become a real cyclist.

And you will miss so much.

Your New Targets

To become a real pilot you now have to achieve these four targets:

1   Carry out a practice emergency diversion. (Consult the Aeronautical Information Circular, "*Use of the VHF International Aeronautical Emergency Service*")

2   Cross three MATZs

3   Fly into and out of three airfields in Class D airspace.

4   Fly to a foreign country and land at three airfields there.

Once you have achieved these targets you may consider yourself a reasonably competent aerial voyager. You will also have acquired the self-confidence to undertake flights from A to B anywhere in Western Europe with pleasurable anticipation rather than the dread which probably accompanied your first solo flights into the unknown. By the time you have achieved these targets you will probably have added at least another fifty hours to your log-book, and maybe a good deal more than that. However, if it is a great deal more than that, I would suggest that you have not been pushing yourself as much as you ought if you are to get the most out of being a PPL holder. Maybe your flying has become a bit too repetitious and unadventurous to be really satisfying. Maybe you would have made better progress if you had teamed up with another pilot and had extended your experience together.

Reaching these targets will make you a more experienced and self-confident pilot than most other PPLs, and indeed you may be surprised to know that you will probably be a more experienced route flyer than some junior instructors. Their world is the world of flying instruction; the circuit, the local flying area and the navex around a handful of very familiar routes. You, on the other hand, have left school now and have moved on to the big world beyond the school gates.

Apart from having learned a good deal more than the PPL syllabus had time to teach you, I guarantee that you will have enjoyed yourself tremendously. So far as the actual flying is concerned you will have enjoyed the satisfaction of preparing for a complex task, anticipating it with understandable trepidation, performing it and ultimately looking back on it with pride. No doubt some mistakes were made *en route,* but you got there without any major upset. You learned a bit more about flying and now you feel thrilled to have successfully made another difficult aerial voyage. You may also now be enjoying the rewards of the traveller, eating foreign foods and seeing strange new places and people – even if you only get as far as the other end of the UK.

In these aerial adventures the attractions of sharing the flight with another pilot become most obvious. A major consideration is the sharing of the cost, but in addition there is the advantage of being able to share the workload; to monitor each other and to form a team which should be far more effective in conducting the flight than either of you would have been solo. If the other pilot has flown the route before, that will be a reassurance for you. But make sure that you take an active part in the proceedings, either as handling pilot or as radio operator/navigator. Just sitting there observing is nowhere near as educational as participating. Some of the better flying schools and clubs organise flyouts to distant airfields as a small group of aircraft, and these can be an excellent way of enlarging your experience and enjoying yourself at the same time. You will have the mutual support and exchange of information at the planning stage, the reassurance of other more experienced pilots accompanying you and the camaraderie of the group with its shared achievement at the destination. If your own flying school does not make much effort in this direction, make inquiries about its rivals. There may be more fun and more useful experiences to be had elsewhere.

Some of the members of the South Warwickshire Flying School on a group flyout to Rouen.
The trip would have taken them less than three hours from Wellesbourne Mountford

Navaids

Navaids

This is a book for VFR pilots and so I do not intend to dwell in any detail on the various navaids which are meat and drink to IFR aviators. The point about flying VFR is meant to be that you spend 98% of your time looking out of the windows, making sure in so doing that you know where you are going and that you do not fly into any other aircraft. It would be perverse to ignore the existence in your cockpit of any navaids, since they may be of material help to you. However, the sensible VFR pilot sees them as no more than aids. The real work is done with the head well out of the office, and any navaids are used only as back-up to visual navigation. If the whole lot packs up it will be a minor inconvenience only, rather than the major emergency it would be to the IFR pilot.

The point is that for the VFR pilot, navaids of any sort are secondary facilities only, the primary facility being visual navigation – whereas for the IFR pilot the navaids are primary. Consequently the IFR pilot has to know a good deal more about the theory and practice of navigational aids than does the VFR pilot.

I shall deal only with the practical application for VFR purposes of navaids, and you should realise that there is much more to learn about them before you could come to put your trust in them unreservedly – i.e. to fly IFR. If you are flying one day as a VFR pilot and find yourself following a track commanded by a navaid but unable to recognise or reconcile the ground which passes below with your map, you have reached a situation where you are using the navaid as the primary navigational reference. As an untrained IFR pilot you are not being prudent, and the proper course is to face the fact that actually you are lost. You should therefore ignore the navaid and institute the usual procedures which you were taught that a VFR pilot should do when lost. You should establish an area of uncertainty and resolve the problem using visual navigation techniques. Having done so, you can always confirm your position using a navaid – but you should rely on visual navigation and not radio nav or GPS to find your position in the first place. An exception to this rule is that you can use radar or the distress service to fix your position and obtain vectors. If being lost presents a potentially serious situation (for instance because of the proximity of controlled airspace or because you are running short of fuel, satisfactory weather and/or daylight) asking for help in good time is the proper course to take. But be sure not to accept any vector which takes you into IMC.

The panel on the PA28 Archer III

Every light aircraft seems to have a different avionics fit, and the same selection of avionics will be set out in a variety of different ways. Often there seems to be a sort of lash-up of a layout and this can be because it represent the culmination over many years of a lengthy series of additions, modifications and further modifications. So whenever you fly an aircraft which is new to you, it is essential that you give yourself half an hour or so of sitting in the cockpit and making quite sure that you know how to select, operate and deselect all the navaids. This is important even if you have no intention of actually using some or all of the aids on the forthcoming flight. The reason for this will soon become clear if you set off without the necessary preparation. Sooner or later you risk discovering that you do not know how to tune the radio to ·025 or ·075 frequencies, or you have selected by mistake some ident or other and you cannot turn it off, or there is intolerable interference from something else which eventually turns out to be the squelch on one of the radios.

I shall describe the standard full IFR fit, but do not imagine that you will find it as described when you get in your next strange aircraft. Expect instead something along these lines with little local variations, perhaps a less complete installation and certainly one with its own special rules of operation. Persuading someone who is familiar with the installation in a particular aircraft to show you around it will save some time, but you must have hands-on experience of selecting, tuning and deselecting everything before you get airborne.

The audio selector

At the heart of every complex avionics fit is the selector box. This is a sort of telephone exchange which allows you to select and deselect the channelling into your headset or the speaker of the sounds issuing forth from the various avionics items which are in use. The conventional audio selector box will have switches for every conceivable facility with "off", "speaker" and/or "phones" options in each case. The radios will be included in the listed facilities and their appropriate switches will govern whether and how their reception

A typical Audio Selector

is to be heard. In addition to the "Com 1" and "Com 2" switches there will probably be switches for "Auto". Transmitting as opposed to receiving by the radios is governed separately and a transmit switch will probably offer "Com 1" and "Com 2" options. When "Auto" is selected, reception from the com set selected for transmitting will be heard automatically, without any need for reception of that box to be selected as well.

Note the following points:

■ The audio selector does not turn the various sets on and off. It merely sends, when an appropriate selection is made, any sound from the selected facility to headset or speaker. If you have not first turned on the appropriate facility, tuned it and adjusted the volume, you will hear nothing when you select it.

■ With the exception of the transmit switch, the selector does not turn off your last selection when you make a new one. And unless you deselect a facility, you will go on hearing whatever you have selected. So either by accident or design, you can have several different sources audible in your headset and/or on the speaker at the same time.

As far as radio is concerned, the usual way of operating with two radios is to set the audio selector so that reception of both sets is "Off". The "Auto" switch is set to "Headset" (or "Speaker" if that is how you wish to hear the them) and the radio actually heard will then be whichever you have set the transmit switch to. Typical practice would then be to start by tuning Com 1 to the Tower frequency and Com 2 to Approach. You then turn the transmit switch to "Com 1" and you will both transmit and receive on that box. When the time comes to switch to Approach you just turn the transmit switch to "Com 2". You will now be transmitting and receiving on box 2, which was already pre-tuned to Approach. While one box is in use, you tune the other box to the next frequency you are likely to need. Then you only have to switch the Tx selector from one box to the other and reception will be changed simultaneously. The individual "Com 1" and "Com 2" reception switches are there in addition to the "Auto" switch in case you want to transmit and receive on one box and simultaneously listen out on the other. This is a useful option when you are using a radar service on one box and also listening to Volmet or the like for your destination weather.

Where you have only one radio, it may have a "flip-flop" facility so that you can select the next frequency in advance and change to it when needed. Whether you fly with two boxes or one with flip-flop, you will find with practice that selection of the next frequency in advance can often turn out to be very advantageous. You can select the next frequency at a quiet moment – possibly as part of a routine FREDA check – and if the frequency change actually comes at a high-workload time you will not find yourself overloaded by this extra demand upon your overstretched attention. If you've got it, use it!

For the navaids, operation of the selector box is usually by way of turning on all the aids (or at least those that you could conceivably require on this particular flight) and selecting "Ident" on each navaid itself. When you want to check a particular ident, select it on the audio selector and the ident will then be heard. Having made the identification you then deselect the navaid on the selector, but leave reception of the ident running on the navaid itself. So if you should want to make another check of the ident from that set, all you have to do is to make another short-term selection of that facility on the audio selector.

VDF

Many a controller has a clever little cathode-ray tube which shows the direction from which every radio call comes, and if you ask them they will tell you from which direction your call is coming from. You can thus establish the direction in which to fly (in still air) to arrive at the airport and/or you can establish a "position line" and know that somewhere along that line is your position.

A VDF set in a control tower. Each radio call automatically gives a read out of its direction on the set

Establishing the direction to fly to the airport is the most popular function. Imagine that your destination is Cranfield. You have no VOR in your aircraft so you cannot use that beacon on the airfield, but they have VDF and you have a radio so you're in business. Your last turning point was Westcott and your nav plot tells you that the track to Cranfield is 048° and the distance is 18nm. Your strategy is to track direct to Cranfield and call them about ten miles out. They may route you in via the Visual Reference Point at Woburn Town, or maybe they will have other ideas. You are a stranger in these parts and in order to comply with whatever joining instructions they may give you, there is clearly a need to know just where you are when you first call them. There is no visual fixing point beneath you but a town is looming up ahead. If it is Leighton Buzzard you are right of track and if it is Milton Keynes you are left. You cannot wait until overhead the town to identify it because that will be too late to make your initial call.

VDF – using a QDM

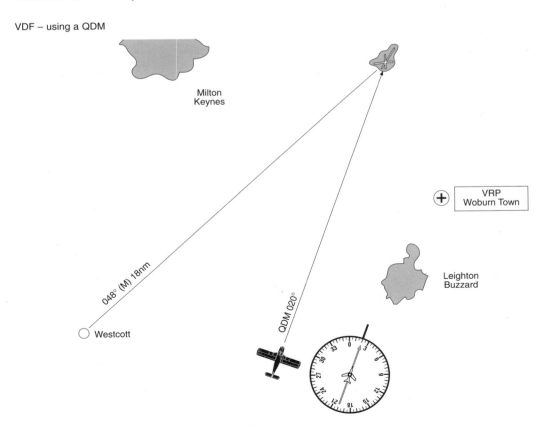

VDF to the rescue! You call Cranfield Approach:

"*QDM QDM. This is G-WOBL, request QDM.*"

They respond:

"*G-WOBL, QDM is 020°*"

You write that down and read back:

"*020°. G-WOBL*"

You now have two useful pieces of information.

1. If you fly 020°(M) in still air, that heading will take you direct to Cranfield: if there is a crosswind today, flying a heading with an appropriate allowance for drift will also take you there direct.

2. Since you need to head a good deal more to the north than the 048° track from Westcott to Cranfield, you must be to the right of track. This being the case, the town ahead must be Leighton Buzzard.

The 'True Bearing' facility provided by VDF is normally used as an *en route* navaid. Imagine that having successfully landed at Cranfield, refuelled, refected and refreshed, you are now on your way to the fair city of Norwich. Cambridge is a few miles ahead and beyond that is the Lakenheath-Mildenhall Combined MATZ (CMATZ). So you are going to have to parley with the USAF for a MATZ crossing. To do this you must once more have an accurate idea of your position – and while there seem to be airfields beneath, it is difficult to distinguish which is which.

So, for further and better information you call Cambridge Approach:

"*True bearing, true bearing. Cambridge, this is G-WOBL, request true bearing*"

Cambridge approach replies:

"*G-WOBL, your true bearing is 270°*"

You read back, as you should always read back figures – and before you do that you write the figures down:

"*G-WOBL, 270°*"

VDF – using a true bearing

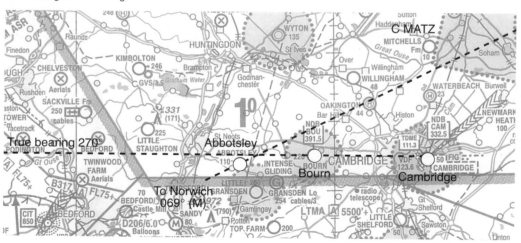

Imagine now a line running at 270°T **from** Cambridge Airport. Somewhere along that line (called a 'Position Line') is your position. This information has not fixed your position but it has substantially reduced your area of uncertainty. It is highly likely that comparing the terrain details which are visible with what the map shows as lying along that imaginary line will fix your position. In this case, amongst the multitude of airfields littering your path across East Anglia, the only ones which appear to lie on that position line and are roughly on your track are Abbotsley and Bourn. If there is a settlement immediately on the north-east edge of the airfield and a dual carriageway starting just two miles to the east, it is Bourn. If the settlement is immediately to the south-west and there is no dual carriageway to the east, it must be Abbotsley.

Radar

To obtain a radar service, all you need is radio – although you will get on much better if you have a transponder as well. All the clever stuff is back in the control room where they have radar screens with the "slugs" depicting each aircraft crawling across. In addition there will be the rotating antennas sending out the pulses and detecting them being bounced back from your aircraft. Radar controllers can "see" a high proportion of aircraft within range whether they have transponders or not, although wooden and GRP aeroplanes tend not to "paint" anything like as well as metal machinery. However, all aircraft are much more easily seen if they are transponder-equipped, and can always be better identified by the controller asking the pilot to "squawk" a particular code assigned at that time by the controller to that aircraft. If you have a transponder with altitude encoding (also known as 'Mode C') the controller will also know at what height you are flying and will therefore be even more comfortable giving you a radar service. If the controller sees two slugs on collision course and both have only Mode A (i.e. they have no altitude information showing), warnings have to be given and aircraft diverted. If they have Mode C, however, the controller may see that there is 1000ft or more between them and no need for any action.

Mode S is the next step up. It is already mandatory for airliners and fully IFR equipped GA aircraft are beginning to sport Mode S boxes in their panels. VFR aircraft will follow. This transponder continually broadcasts the aircraft's registration, type, height and other basic details.

With the arrival in European skies of airliners and other aircraft fitted with TCAS (Traffic alert and Collision Avoidance System) there is all the more need for transponders to have height reporting. Otherwise airliners flying perhaps tens of thousands of feet higher than you and I may have to take sudden avoiding action to avoid a falsely anticipated collision.

The radar service most used by VFR pilots is the Lower Airspace Radar Service, and a wonderful facility it is too – especially on weekdays when the military take part. At weekends, alas, it is more patchy. On offer are either a Radar Information Service (RIS) or a Radar Advisory Service (RAS) and you will be asked which you require. The RIS gives you information about other aircraft in the vicinity and leaves you to find them and seek your own way around them. As this is what VFR pilots are doing all the time in any case, this fits the bill nicely. So for VFR purposes you must choose the RIS and leave the RAS to those in IMC and unable to look out for themselves.

To use a radar service you call the appropriate LARS and give a full position and route report, ending:

> "Request Radar Information Service."

The controller will give you a squawk code to select, which you will write down, read back and then select. If you have no transponder you will say:

> "G-WOBL negative squawk"

The controller may then ask you to fly a particular heading so as to identify your aircraft You may then wish that you did have a transponder, as the excursion from track is going to complicate your navigation if it goes on for long.

Once the controller has identified you, a further call will come:

> "G-WOBL, you are identified. Radar Information Service at Flight Level 35."

You read back the type of service agreed and the level.

If you cannot be identified, perhaps because of being too low or too far away, the controller may offer you a Flight Information Service to be going on with. When you come within range of the radar you will be told that the RIS has now begun.

Sometimes the controller will tell you that you are in or about to enter an area where there is too much traffic for you to be warned of individual aircraft, but you may be told the location of a particular concentration of them. For example;

> *"G-BL, there are numerous traces in the vicinity of Lasham, probably glider activity"*

The main purpose of the service is to avoid mid-air collisions and reports of other aircraft nearby are usually welcome. The R/T traffic usually goes something like this:

"G-BL, traffic in your ten o'clock, four miles, left to right, reporting height four thousand feet."

You reply either:

> *"G-BL, looking."* or
> *"G-BL, traffic in sight."*

Once the controller knows that you are "visual" with the other traffic, the need to monitor a potential collision will cease. So a traffic-in-sight report is always welcome to the controller.

On a busy day you may receive several reports of traffic which you never actually see, and at times you may wonder if the controller thinks that you have nothing better to do than search the horizon for invisible aircraft. However, it is better to have too much information than not enough. And if the controller's voice rises in pitch as you are informed that the previously reported traffic is now two miles ahead in your one o'clock and closing, you may find yourself taking a particularly keen interest in the reports and the sky outside.

The Radar Service has other useful benefits as well as collision avoidance. You only have to ask and they will tell you your position, and that is sometimes a great boon. Furthermore they can easily tell you how to get to your next waypoint:

> *"G-BL, request vector to Newport."*
> *"G-BL, steer 065 for Newport."*
> *"G-BL, 065."*

(You did write that heading down before you read it back, didn't you?)

If they are not busy they can smooth the way ahead for you:

> *"Brize Radar, G-BL, could you please contact Yeovil to say that I shall be with them at 1705Z and ask whether will they still be open then? "*

Last but by no means least, they can watch out for you and keep you out of trouble. There have been many times in my own flying career when Radar has piped up with something along the lines of:

> *"G-BL, to avoid controlled airspace, descend to 2400ft."*

In most of these cases I have been aware of the upcoming controlled airspace and was planning to commence a descent shortly in any case; I do like to hang on to altitude for as long as I can. In some instances, however, I must confess to having overlooked the approaching controlled airspace and it has only been the timely reminder of Radar which has saved me from my own incompetence. If you are one of those supremely efficient pilots who never forgets any little detail, never let distractions lead to oversights and are generally infallible, the bonus which radar offers is of no particular interest. But if, like me, you are somewhat less than perfect, having someone watch over your progress is an enormously useful back-up.

With ever increasing controller shortage and severe commercial pressures on air traffic service providers it is sometimes difficult, these days, to obtain a Radar Information Service (RIS) and you may well find yourself being told either that only a limited cover can be offered or that no service can be provided. A further pressure on hard stretched controllers is the issue of personal liability. While controllers will probably want to help when asked, they will be aware of the fact that if a mid air was to occur to an aircraft under a RIS, and they had given insufficient warning of its possibility, they will be in deep trouble. They are reluctant, therefore to provide a service when there is a possibility of becoming overloaded and unable to maintain sufficient watch. With such controllers some sort of service can often be obtained by asking for a Flight Information Service. You will probably be given a discrete code by a radar controller in any case and they will probably keep an eye out for you.

The NDB and ADF

NDB stands for 'Non-Directional Beacon' and ADF for 'Automatic Direction Finding'. The NDB is the ground equipment and the ADF is what you have in your aircraft. Fifty years ago this was state-of-the-art kit. It usually appears on your panel as a box for tuning and selecting facilities and, separately, a dial showing a compass rose with a needle superimposed. The most common dial presentation used in VFR aircraft is the Relative Bearing Indicator (RBI). This performs the simple function of having a needle which always points towards the beacon, wherever it is. The compass rose on the instrument dial is sometimes fixed. However, if you find that you can rotate it with a knob at the side, set it so that north is uppermost. It will then be just the same as the instrument with the fixed rose.

To use the ADF you first tune it to your selected NDB's frequency. This can be found either from a flight guide or from your map. An NDB is shown on the map by concentric circles of blue dots and the frequency will have three digits with, occasionally, a decimal five on the end. Your ADF tuning will not provide for half digits so try either side and see which gives the best signal. Having tuned in the signal, you must now check that what you have got is indeed the desired NDB. These beacons occupy an area of the radio spectrum between the long and medium-wave bands on your radio set back home, and under certain conditions it is perfectly possible to receive a transmitter quite different from the one you wanted. Indeed, an ADF receiver is quite capable of being tuned to an LW or MW broadcasting station and giving a bearing to it, although you should not use it in this way. Each NDB has its own identifying code of two or three letters and the beacon transmits these in Morse code. If you don't know Morse, look up the identifier and write on your flight log at flight-preparation stage the appropriate Morse characters for each beacon whose frequency you list. If you are within range of an NDB and cannot hear the identifier, try selecting 'BFO' on the ADF. This will improve identification of some NDBs, but not all.

Having tuned and identified your NDB, see if the needle swings positively towards the beacon. If in doubt, test the kit by turning off the direction-seeking function (often by turning the selector switch from ADF to ANT, for antenna). The needle should swing away and wander. Turn direction-seeking back on and the needle should swing back to the original direction.

Bear in mind the restricted range of this aid. An NDB is not usually very reliable at more than about ten miles range, even when the published range is more. Also you must always bear in mind the possibility of inaccuracy caused by coastal and night effects, thunderstorms and other things.

Using an NDB is often a useful way of checking progress along track. "At 1028 we should get GY abeam on our right-hand side", you think to yourself – or you tell the handling pilot, if you are currently doing the radio and navigation only. So at 1020 you should have GY tuned and identified. It should be showing a relative bearing somewhere in your one or two o'clock (somewhere around 045° on the RBI) but don't spend time dwelling upon the figure. Just remember that the needle always points to the beacon, and imagine that someone is sitting in the back seat and continually pointing a finger in the direction of the beacon. If your ADF needle is pointing roughly in the right direction, all is going well. If it's not, you have something important to look into.

Sometimes an NDB is useful as a position fix and/or a waypoint. Westcott near Aylesbury is a popular example, being a reporting point for the airways system at FL55 and above but not part of any airfield approach procedure below. Of course, its very popularity makes it a place where lookout is at a premium...

A typical ADF set and its associated Relative Bearing Indicator

NDB Exercise

Choose a suitable NDB, and note its frequency and ident. If it forms part of an airfield's approach pattern, phone ATC and explain that you want to do a VFR exercise involving the beacon. Tell them roughly what this will entail and agree when and how this will be convenient for them.

Position yourself about 15nm from the beacon, tune to it, identify it and then turn the aircraft around until the needle is pointing straight up at about 360° give or take about 5°. Do not let yourself become fascinated by the needle and anxious to nail it exactly on the 360° mark because it will swing about a fair bit – and in any case, remember that the NDB is not a very accurate aid anyway. Visualise having someone in the cockpit beside you pointing in the direction of the needle (straight ahead in this case) and telling you that the beacon is somewhere over *there* but they are not sure how far away. Now fly towards where the man is pointing. You do this like a good VFR pilot should, by choosing an appropriate landmark and flying towards it. Check the needle every mile or so and correct your heading by choosing a new landmark as appropriate. A significant crosswind will blow you across track in the same way that it would on an approach to landing. So you aim off a bit to counteract the crosswind.

Note that you do not have any indication of how far away the beacon is unless you can visually identify a ground feature, but you do know that you are somewhere on a line which leads towards the beacon. And you know the direction of that "position line" because it is the direction of your track. So if you are tracking a shade west of north-west, for instance, imagine a line of that approximate direction passing through the NDB and be aware that you are somewhere on it and flying towards the beacon. This should make identifying a ground feature that much easier.

As you approach the beacon you may notice that the needle alters its indication much more quickly. Eventually it will swing rapidly around to point behind you. At this stage you will know that you have flown over – or very close to – the beacon, and thus you now have a position fix. Note the time of your fix, which might be useful navigational information later.

So using the NDB you have first established yourself on a known position line from which you may well make a positive visual fix, and then you have obtained a radio fix by overflying the beacon.

The VOR

Description

The VOR is a rather more sophisticated navaid than the NDB although it is also quite antique, representing the state-of-the-art of the late 1950s. It has considerably greater usable range; in theory it is line-of-sight from the beacon, although each beacon's maximum usable range is given in the AIP. VOR does not suffer from the variety of errors to which ADF is prone and in principle offers accuracy to within 5° or so. Furthermore it will tell you when it is not receiving either a proper VOR signal or one able to offer reliable navigational information. In this it differs markedly from an ADF receiver, which if mistuned is quite happy to point to BBC Radio Guernsey when all the time you thought it was pointing at GRB. It also does not suffer from the ADF's tendency to substitute the nearest thunderstorm for the tuned-in NDB.

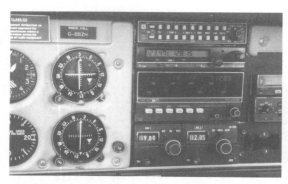

Two VORs and their associated CDIs. Both needles are centralised on radials of about 029 FROM a VOR on the frequency of 112.05

While the NDB has a needle in the cockpit which always points to the beacon, the VOR presents its information in a rather more obscure manner. In essence the VOR transmitter sends out 360 'radials' from the beacon. The cockpit instrumentation allows you to select any one of them and then tells you whether you are on it or, if not, whether you should fly left or right in relation to that radial to capture it.

The VOR beacon on the ground operates in the VHF range, as does the ordinary aircraft radio. In the cockpit you will usually find a tuning and selection box. This is often partnered with a radio set and the two are referred to as a "Com-Nav". An aircraft fully equipped for instrument flying will have two com-nav sets, "Box 1" and "Box 2". The radios will be "Com 1" and "Com 2" and the VORs will be "Nav 1" and "Nav 2". In addition to the tuning and selection box there will be, for each Nav, a dial with a 'Course Deviation Indicator' (CDI). This comprises a dial with a vertical needle or bar which can travel from left to right across the dial and over a small circle positioned in the centre. When the needle or bar is over the circle, your aircraft is over the selected VOR radial. If you are within ten degrees of the selected radial, the needle or bar will take up an intermediate position on the dial. If you are more than ten degrees out, the needle or bar will go right to the stop on one side or the other.

Around the edge of the dial is a rotatable compass rose with a window and a mark at the top of the instrument. In the bottom left-hand corner of the dial is a knob which is known as the 'Omni Bearing Selector' (OBS). By turning the OBS you rotate the rose; the value on the rose which you set against the mark on the top is the radial which you have selected. At the bottom of the instrument is another window in which you will be able to read off the reciprocal of the selected radial at any time.

If the instrument also offers a glideslope indication for the 'Instrument Landing System' (ILS) there will also be a horizontal needle or bar with a vertical scale. This need not concern a VFR pilot – but just for your information, it tells you your vertical position in relation to the glideslope when flying an ILS approach. With or without ILS you will see a TO and a FROM arrow or indication when the instrument is tuned to a VOR. You will see only one of them at any one time.

Finally, the instrument has "flags", and these tell you whether the reading is reliable or not. The flags take various forms depending upon the avionics manufacturer. Sometimes the only flag amounts to the absence of either TO or FROM indicators, and on other units there is a more obvious indication. Whatever it may be, you will see it whenever the instrument is switched off. The flags are one of the great advantages which VOR offers over ADF. With ADF you can never be entirely sure that the indication is dependable, but if the VOR "flags" are "away" you are entitled to expect accuracy within five degrees.

Operation

It is important to be careful and methodical in using the VOR. If you are not, it will be easy to mistakenly set the aid. If the result is that the flags indicate no usable signal, that will be merely irritating. However, if you tune to a usable but incorrect signal you will then be seriously misled. Proceed thus:

1. Switch on the instrument, turn down the volume and select ident.

2. Tune to the frequency of the desired beacon.

3. Check the ident. In an extensively equipped aircraft this will probably entail selecting "Nav 1" or "2" on the audio box. Increase the ident volume to a comfortable level and check that you are hearing the appropriate Morse group. (You turn the volume down at first because sometimes the volume has been set by a previous pilot to near maximum to hear a weak ident. If the next selected ident comes in at strength five, you and your passengers are going to get an unpleasant surprise.)

4. Check that the flags are away.

5. Adjust the OBS as required.

Things usually go wrong with use of the VOR either because the wrong frequency is selected (or you imagine you have selected it when you are actually still on the old one) or because the wrong OBS is selected, or because TO is confused with FROM. So you need to check that everything is set up as it should be before you use this aid. FIFO is a useful mnemonic:

> **F**requency selected.
> **I**dent checked.
> **F**lags away.
> **O**BS set.

Interpreting the VOR

Just remember that if you twiddle the OBS until the CDI needle is in the centre, the VOR tells you on which radial you are currently situated. This is quite irrespective of which way you happen to be pointing at the time, and is the essential difference between VOR and ADF.

Having centred the CDI, the OBS reading at the top of the instrument shows you the track TO the beacon if the TO flag is showing. If FROM is being indicated, the instrument is showing you the track diametrically away from the beacon (i.e. the radial from the beacon).

If you want to track directly towards a VOR from your present position, centre the needle with the OBS and with TO showing. Note the track shown at the top of the instrument, make any appropriate adjustment for crosswind and fly the resulting heading. The needle or bar now represents your desired track line. If it starts wandering off to the left, that means the track is wandering off to the left as well. You should therefore adjust your heading to the left a touch. Remember that you always turn *towards* the bar or needle to recapture it, and the bar represents your desired track line rather than the centre marking on the instrument.

If you want to fly a track directly away from a beacon, follow the same procedure but centre the CDI with the FROM flag showing. This of course will be the exact reciprocal of the TO value.

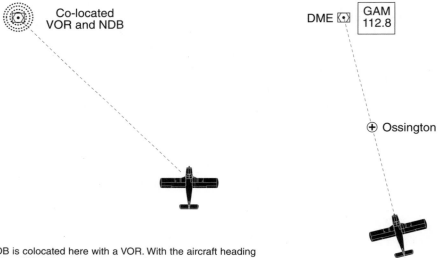

An NDB is colocated here with a VOR. With the aircraft heading north the ADF needle will show about 315° Any change in the aircraft's heading will cause an equivalent change in the direction taken up by the needle. On the VOR, however, the heading of the aircraft is irrelevant. If you twiddle the OBS until the CDI is central with a TO indication, you will get a reading of around 315°

Finding Ossington using the GAM VOR's 166° Radial. Once you are on that radial you are on a position line which passes through Ossington

If there is a particular track along which you wish to fly to or from a beacon, set the required track on the OBS and fly a track which will cross the selected radial. As you get within ten degrees of the track, the needle or bar will leave the stop at the side and start to traverse across the dial. As it approaches the centre you are coming up to the required radial and can then continue TO or FROM as above.

Interpreting the VOR can be rather confusing at times, and teachers of instrument flying sometimes delight in putting difficult interpretation scenarios to students. For VFR pilots it is best to keep things as simple as possible. So if you are ever unsure as to just what the instrument is telling you, centre the OBS with FROM showing and look at the map (which conveniently has a compass rose aligned with magnetic north superimposed on top of every VOR). What the aid is telling you is simply that your present position is somewhere along the radial indicated at the top of the instrument.

A VOR will do all that an NDB will do but more effectively. Apart from overhead and abeam positioning, you can conveniently use the radials from a VOR. Say you choose the disused airfield at Ossington, near the Gamston VOR in Nottinghamshire, as a waypoint on your route. You note on your flight log as part of your preparations that Ossington lies on the 166° radial FROM Gamston. Tune in to Gamston in good time, identify and set the OBS to 166°. When the CDI is central, you know that you are on the position line from Gamston which passes through Ossington. If it's not beneath you, either fly away from Gamston – keeping the CDI central – or fly towards it to locate Ossington.

If you can arrange a route so that a VOR lies on or close to your track, you can use the VOR to maintain track. So to track from Ossington to Netherthorpe, which being grass and small is not easy for a stranger to find, you might elect to route overhead Gamston VOR (remember either to fly above the Retford ATZ – up to 2000ft AAL – or around it, and to give them a call). From Gamston you need only to maintain the 289° radial and to time your leg from Gamston to locate Netherthorpe.

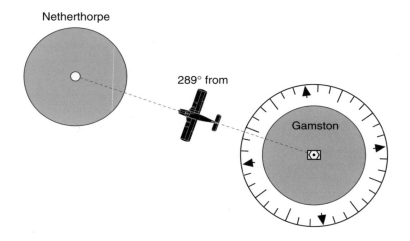

With two VORs or one VOR and an NDB, you can fix your position by cross bearings. However, this is in my view too complicated for a single pilot to attempt in the air unless the bearings have been noted at the time of flight preparation. If they have, the strategy is simply to fly down one position line until the cross-bearing from the other facility comes up. Even then, if one facility is an NDB the operation may well be far too taxing for a VFR pilot. If both are VORs, you need two such instruments on board because retuning from one frequency to the other and back again on just one instrument creates too much navigational workload for the single pilot – whose time would be much better spent with the head well out of the office.

With VOR co-located with DME (Distance Measuring Equipment) you have a seriously useful aid. The DME will usually have its own separate box from the nav set. This will offer you a tuning facility, and will often make it possible to flip between either groundspeed or time at this speed to reach the beacon. If you tune to a VOR/DME, you can establish your position anywhere within range by using the radial and distance. For single-pilot operation it's *not* a good idea to try drawing radial lines from the VOR on your map while flying. You can visually gauge the radial line easily enough, using the compass rose imposed by the map-makers on the VOR. Distance can usually be judged visually using guesstimation techniques. For instance, the diameter of a MATZ is 10nm and there is usually one on some part of the map. And if it's the usual half-mil, your thumb is about 10nm and a hand-span about 50nm. It's helpful to have your pencils marked with cuts at 5 and 10nm intervals to measure longer distances. Or failing that, you can measure your pencil against the latitude marks on the map, hold your fingers or your pencil against the distance measured and then measure the same amount from the VOR. The important principle is not to get too bogged down in detail when you are piloting. Keep everything simple if approximate.

My father was captain of the village Home Guard during the Second World War, and as an exercise his platoon defended their village against attack by the platoon from the neighbouring village. He and his sergeant pored over maps laid on a convenient tombstone in the church graveyard ("They wus doin thur maps", an ancient and rustic former member of the platoon explained to me some twenty years later). But while they were thus engaged in the important matter of making their military dispositions, the entire attacking platoon tiptoed past them and captured the church which was their headquarters. Since then, my family has had a preference for looking about themselves rather than "doing thur maps" and that is a very good principle for the single pilot as well.

A highly practical use for the VOR/DME is to arrange your route so that you fly along a radial and use the DME to tell you how far there is to go and when you will be there. Alternatively, you can fly a radius around a DME and use the radial to establish your position. Flying a radius around a DME is easier than you might think provided that you use a minimum of about eight miles, otherwise the heading corrections become too frequent for simplicity. With only a little practice you will find that proficiency is soon acquired.

This is how to go about it. Let's say that you want to fly a ten-mile radius around a DME. Proceed by whatever method is convenient to a point about ten miles from the facility. By twiddling the OBS, find out what radial you are on. Turn to a heading which is 90° either more or less than the radial. That will set you flying across the radial line. Note where you are pointing against some external marker towards the horizon and don't look at your heading indicator again. The thing here is that you are a visual pilot and you need not, must not, spend valuable time looking in when you could be looking out. Anyway, it is far easier to fly towards some distant visual mark than it is to chase the HI.

Let's say that your heading at 90° to the radial leaves you pointing just to the left of a big wood, and let's assume that you turned on to a heading which puts the VOR/DME beacon on your right-hand side. Check the DME reading. If it is more than the required 10nm, turn towards the beacon; if it is less, turn away from it. How much should you turn? Well, it depends on how big a correction is called for and you will not really know that until you have seen what sort of difference your first correction makes. For a start, try a ten-degree correction (remember, no looking at the HI). In this example, let's assume that your DME reading is now 10·7nm, so you need to turn right 10°. So make an intelligent guess as to where "ten degrees right" of your previous marker will leave you pointing and head for that instead. Continue with regular checks and corrections as you fly around the radius. For a 10nm radius, DME checks about every thirty seconds will suffice and subsequent corrections should never be more than 10° left or right of your immediately previous heading. This method is quite accurate enough for visual flying, and indeed something very similar is favoured by many instrument pilots for flying a radius around a DME.

In the case of the leg from Ossington to Netherthorpe using VOR/DME, you might plan this leg so that you leave Ossington on a track of 292° (T). At this point your DME distance from GAM will be about 6nm. As you pass tangentially south abeam GAM, the DME will decrease to about 5nm and then start to increase as you draw away from the beacon. You are looking for 9nm, which is the distance from Netherthorpe to GAM. When the DME gives about 8nm, check the radial – which will be about 260° – and turn to a heading of (260 + 90) = 350°. Maintain a DME reading of about 9nm and set the OBS to 290°. When the CDI is in the middle, you are overhead Netherthorpe.

This strategy, which is available only if you have DME as well as VOR, has the great advantage of not requiring you to fly overhead GAM for your position fix before the final run-in to Netherthorpe. This has significant safety implications because the overheads of VORs and NDBs are quite popular places. This is especially the case amongst aircraft flown by pilots very busy just at that time with assorted chores; setting new headings, noting the time, calculating the next ETA, retuning navaids and generally doing anything rather than look out for other aircraft being flown by similarly preoccupied pilots. Beacon overheads are places to avoid if at all possible, and with DME you can.

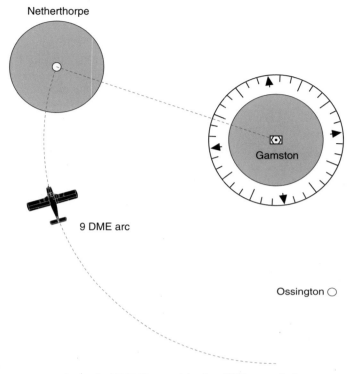

Finding Netherthorpe using the GAM VOR/DME. Fly round the 9nm DME arc and when you reach the 289° radial, you are overhead

VOR Exercises

The more you use the aid, the more familiar with it you will become and the more use it will be to you. Start by working out how to fly towards and away from a beacon, much as you did with the NDB. Be sure to follow the FIFO procedure religiously. If you don't, you would be safer not using VOR at all.

Next, try picking up a radial. Visualise a radial line from a local VOR which passes five or ten miles away from your present position. Alternatively, draw such a line on your map before you take off and navigate yourself to a point some five or ten miles away. Now you have to fly to a point somewhere on that radial line, using the VOR indications to guide you. Do your FIFO procedure and set the OBS to the value of the direction of the radial line. Let's assume that it is at 225° FROM the VOR, and let's also assume that our position is such that if we fly roughly north-east, we reckon that we shall cut the desired radial at about 90°.

Now flying a track to give a 90° cut will give you the quickest way to get to the desired radial line, but sometimes other considerations will cause you to seek some other more oblique cut. In such cases you will alter your track to left or right of the 90° cut track as required. For a start, fly this track and observe how, as you get close to your desired radial line, the CDI needle will leave the stop on one side of the instrument and move towards the midpoint. Recall that this indicates that you are now positioned on the desired radial line. Now try tracking along the radial. If you are tracking away from the beacon, turn on to a heading which is the same as the radial. FROM will show on the CDI and the needle will indicate where your desired track has got to. If the needle is out to the left of the instrument, your track is to the left. So try a heading of about 15° to the left of (or less than) the radial value. Choose a visual marker towards the horizon which will give you the new heading and fly towards it. After 30 seconds or so, check the CDI to see where your desired track has got to. Make appropriate adjustments of your heading from time to time to capture and maintain the desired track.

If you waited until the needle was central before turning when you were approaching the desired radial on your 90° cut, you would have overshot by the time you had turned on to the radial heading. So you need to anticipate a little and start the turn on to the radial before the needle is central.

If you are tracking towards the beacon rather than away from it, you should twiddle the OBS to the reciprocal of the radial value and fly so that TO is showing on the CDI. In this way the desired track will be represented by the needle, as before. If, however, you leave the radial value set on the OBS and then fly to the beacon when the CDI is reading FROM, you will get reverse readings from the needle. So when tracking a radial, be very careful as part of your FIFO procedure to check that you are getting a TO reading when flying towards the beacon and a FROM when flying away from it. If you are not, you haven't set up the OBS correctly.

If you set out to capture a radial when you are close to the beacon, and especially if you are using a 90° cut, you will find that you fly through the "window" of 10° either side of the radial rather quickly. Using our old friend the 1 in 60 rule, let me demonstrate:

Distance from beacon = 5nm. Cut = 90°

Angle subtended by 1nm = 1° x 60/5 = 12°

The distance subtended by the twenty-degree "window" of the CDI is therefore less than 2nm at 5nm from the beacon, and this will take only about 45 seconds to fly through in the average light aeroplane. Remember that for the remaining 340° of the circle around the VOR, the needle of the CDI will rest on the stops. Only by changing the OBS setting or moving the position of the aircraft will you persuade the needle to move. Forty-five seconds is not a very long time in which to notice the needle of the CDI if you happen to be distracted by something else at the time. You could double this time available by altering the cut to 45°, or you could also double it if you captured the radial at ten miles out instead of five.

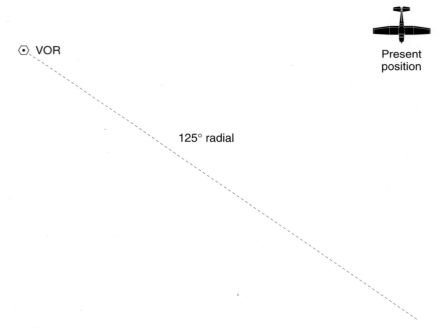

Present position

VOR

125° radial

Picking up a VOR radial

Step 1. Establish your position in relation to VOR. You may already know this, but if not, twiddle the OBS until you have centred the CDI with FROM showing. The reading at the top of the rose is the radial you are currently on from VOR (about 085° in this case). Look at the map and know that you are somewhere on that position line

Step 2. Decide what track to fly to cross the 125° Radial. The quickest track, but not always the best, will be at 90° to the desired radial – 215° in this case. This is called "a 90° cut"

Step 3. Fly your chosen track. In the above case with the OBS set to the desired 125°, the CDI will remain on the right hand stop until you are within 10° of your selected radial when it will leave the stop and move across until it is central when you are on the125° radial

Another way of giving yourself more time is to move the OBS setting towards the desired radial in increments. You centralise the needle when at your original position by twiddling the OBS. Suppose that your desired radial is 225°, as before, and you find that you are currently on the 190° radial. Alter the OBS to 10° closer to your desired radial, which is 200°. This makes the needle just active and you can monitor its progress from one side of the scale to the other, by which time you will have reached the 210° radial. Reset the OBS to 220° and when the needle has moved across halfway towards the centre, reset again to the desired 225° for your final capture of the radial. This method gives you more notice of the arrival of the radial, more awareness of the speed at which you are approaching it, and − because of the need to readjust the OBS from time to time − it keeps your eye on the CDI.

There are more sophisticated ways of capturing a radial but these are really the province of the instrument pilot. The VOR is not always easy to interpret and the VFR pilot would do well to keep things simple. Just remember:

1   If you centralise the needle with FROM showing, the CDI will show you your present radial from the beacon.

2   If you fly towards the beacon with TO showing, or away from the beacon with FROM showing, the needle will represent where your desired track has got to. So you should alter your heading somewhat towards that track.

The VOR is a very useful navaid, but it does need care in use and also needs practice to familiarise yourself with its interpretation. So always observe religiously the FIFO procedure, and keep yourself current in the use of the aid by using it to back up your visual navigation even when you are quite sure of your position anyway.

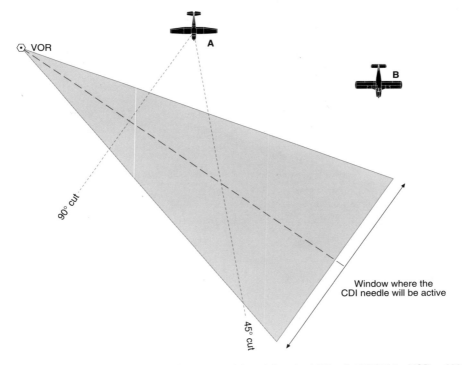

If you are at Position A, close to the beacon, and your wish is to follow the 125° radial FROM the VOR, a 90° cut (215° track) may present difficulties. The window where the needle will be active will be narrow and a rather sharp turn may be required to capture the desired 125° track. A 45° cut (170° track) may make things easier

Farther out from the beacon though, at Position B, a 45° cut (170° track) may take too long and the 90° cut (215° track) may be better. Once the needle becomes active it may be a good plan to reduce the cut and so reduce the amount of final turn required

On the other hand, if you were at Position B and you wished to track TO the beacon rather than FROM, a 45° cut, but in the other direction (ie 260° track) would get you to the beacon more quickly than a 90° cut would. In this instance you would first set the OBS to the reciprocal of 125° (305°) and expect to see TO on the CDI

Area Navaids

Area Navaids

Apart from radar, the navaids described in the last chapter all give information in relation to a fixed point; a radio beacon in the cases of NDB, VOR and DME and a controller's receiver in the case of VDF. These aids work well provided that you are flying directly to or from the relevant beacon, which is why they tend to be placed at convenient points throughout the airways system. While they offer all you need to fly the traditional airways, navigating from one beacon to the next, they are of less immediate value to someone such as the VFR pilot who flies off airways.

So-called 'area' navaids, on the other hand, are not tied directly to beacons. All will tell you your current position and, if you feed in the appropriate co-ordinates of a selected waypoint, they will generate track, distance, groundspeed and estimated elapsed time to that waypoint. Decca was for many years a popular area navaid and Loran is another in common use in the United States, but both have now been replaced by satellite navigation (Satnav).

At the time of writing (2004) the only Satnav facility in Western Europe is the American Global Positioning Satellite (GPS) system but Galileo, the European equivalent, will be with us before very long, which is why I am using the generic title of Satnav rather than GPS. There are other Satnav systems already in Russia and the Far East.

Area navigation or RNAV using VOR, DME and an internal computer is found on the panel in many light aircraft. The current generation of these sets, sometimes known as 'VOR shifters', are currently facing compulsory obsolescence, at least for IFR and as far as the most popular installations are concerned. In the shorter term this is because of their inability to meet the FM broadcast immunity requirements and the 8·33 kHz channel spacing which is becoming mandatory by degrees for European airspace. However, they may still be usable for VFR and in a few cases they may also be capable of modification to meet the new standards of bandwidth. In the longer term, however, the VOR system is doomed to eventual extinction throughout Europe. Leaving that problem aside, RNAV is a good system except that it can be used only when in range of the selected VOR/DME. At height that will not present much problem in the UK because there is nearly always a suitable facility within range. At low level, however, that is often not the case and the VFR pilot seeking navigational help when flying below a low cloudbase is likely to find RNAV no longer available just when it is most needed.

A relatively cheap hand held GPS with a small moving map facility, limited database, temporary aerial and velcro knee attachment. A valuable navigational tool, provided that you use some other navigation system as a check

Without doubt it is Satnav which is the area navaid *par excellence* for the VFR pilot. This is a field where developments come rapidly and today's top-of-the-range kit soon becomes tomorrow's basic specification. The present state of play is that the field is divided into panel-mounted and hand-held units, with a further division into those with a moving-map facility and those without. A few have approval in Europe for IFR use and such units have a self-checking facility such as 'Receiver Autonomous Integrity Monitoring' (RAIM). While all Satnavs will tell you if they have inadequate satellite contact, Satnavs fitted with RAIM and the like constantly monitor their own accuracy and report if they are failing to achieve the required standard. Thus, information from an IFR-approved Satnav can be relied upon while that from unapproved Satnav can only be used to confirm your primary navigation – which for a VFR pilot will be visual navigation. It is unlikely that any handheld Satnav will be approved for IFR in the near future, but so far Satnav has an impressive record for confounding pessimistic predictions about its future as a primary navaid.

Satnav – The Theory

Like DME, Satnav is based on distance measuring. But unlike DME, it measures the distance to several sources rather than just one – and the sources in this case are not stationary beacons but moving satellites. The system therefore depends upon the well-tried principles of triangulation. You could use the same principle to fix your position by using the distance from three DMEs. The circles of ranges around each beacon would intersect at your position. So it is with the ranges around the satellites being used, although in this case we are dealing with spheres of range rather than circles. This is why Satnav can give you height information as well as position. Helpfully arranged in space around our planet are numerous satellites. Each continuously broadcasts its position and the time of each broadcast. Although the technicalities are a shade complicated, in essence your Satnav receiver notes the position of each satellite whose broadcast it receives and compares the time of reception with the time of transmission. The rest is mere arithmetic. The time difference applied to the speed of radio waves allows your Satnav to calculate the distance of that satellite. Receive the signal from three or more satellites in convenient positions, apply the principles of spherical trigonometry – meat and drink to a computer – and lo! you have your position in relation to the earth's surface including your height above it. Because the whole system depends on the measurement of very small periods of time, it is vital that a Satnav receiver is extremely accurate as to the current time and we're talking femtoseconds here. The Satnav in your cockpit has a clock which is accurate over short periods, and it is kept accurate over longer periods by time checks from the atomic clocks on board the satellites.

Satellite Navigation – The Practice

The first thing to be said about Satnav is that it can be extraordinarily accurate. Accuracy within around 2 metres is possible, which would be accurate enough for instrument approaches were it not for the second thing to be said about Satnav, which is that it is unreliable. While the first point is universally recognised, the second is sometimes characterised as being akin to the shaking of the white haired heads of sundry tired old has-beens, unable or unwilling to drag themselves into the technology of the 21st century. To disabuse yourself of this view you should read Safety Sense Leaflet No 25, Information and Guidance to Pilots for the use of GPS in Light Aircraft. You can find this, along with all the other Safety Sense Leaflets published by the CAA, at the back of the current issue of LASORS or on their website. (Until they get their website organised on a more rational footing, the route from www.caa.co.uk is via Safety – General Aviation – Safety Sense Leaflets. The 'Publications' box on the Home Page is there just to mislead you.) The leaflet lists several ways in which the system itself, as opposed to the operator, can lead you astray you. In many of these cases there will be no way that you, the pilot will know that anything is amiss, and that the customary 10m accuracy has now degraded to, say, two miles. This ought to be enough to convince you of the unwisdom of using Satnav as a means of carrying out unofficial IFR or marginal VFR approaches. One day will be your unlucky day and you may not realise this until it is too late.

What you might call the 'first generation' of Satnav sets had a moving map if it had one at all, that lacked sufficient screen size and topographical detail to be of much practical use. The second generation sets are now beginning to appear in some cockpits and flight bags and these have a screen size of at least 5 ins diagonally across and a colour map which replicates a 1:500,000 topo or at least get very close to it in detail, including terrain heights and contours. The Bendix/King Skymap IIIC is a good example and others are becoming available. I should categorise any set with a smaller screen or lesser topographical detail as being inadequate for 'second generation' status. While an IFR Satnav set, such as the Garmin 530 offers a reasonable size of screen, the database offers insufficient topographical detail, in my opinion, to qualify as a 'second generation' VFR set. Furthermore it lacks a joystick for moving the cursor around and the alternative offered of using concentric knobs is a good deal less easy to use in the air.

The 'first generation' set, although enormously better than nothing, presents substantial problems as regards its use in a reliable manner and these problems arise largely because of the way locations are presented. With a second generation set a position is accurately displayed at all times on the moving map with navigational figures alongside. When you want to define the next, or any, waypoint you can simply move a cursor across the map to tell the set where you want to go. Without this facility, however, the 'first generation' set is reduced to defining waypoints in user unfriendly ways. The principal method among these is by using lat/long co-ordinates, which is tedious, tortuous and non intuitive. Worst of all, it is highly prone to operator error and wrongly entering just one of the 15 required digits can be disastrous. While wrongly inputting 'S' instead of 'N' will probably produce navigational information that is patently absurd, so that you will check for wrong inputs, an error in one of the numbers may send you off on a track only, say, ten degrees off. At first this will make no appreciable difference, but in time it may easily lead you to an unauthorised penetration of the very controlled airspace that you had thought that you were so cleverly avoiding.

The chances of wrongly inputting a digit while flying your aircraft are high, while the chances of your flying your aircraft competently while inputting lat/long co-ordinates are virtually nil and consequently you should never attempt to input co-ordinates while flying your aircraft. The most that the single pilot/navigator can hope to achieve with a first generation satnav set while flying is to navigate by whatever waypoints are already in the set's database. Once you are airborne it is too late to try to add to the database, and that is a task for the ground only.

An aviation satnav set will be sold with a database that will probably include all licensed airfields, identified by their ICAO code, and radio beacons, identified by their ident letters. It may also include airways reporting points but as these are not shown on a topo map, they are of little use to the VFR pilot. A database that included Visual Reporting Points (VRPs) around airfields would be very much more useful to a VFR pilot.

You can add to your set's database by adding User Waypoints and in this way you can greatly improve the value of the set to you in the air. If you enter into the User Waypoint list at the flight planning stage all the likely waypoints on a proposed route (other than any already forming part of the set's fixed database) you can then summon up any of these waypoints from the list as and when needed.

When entering the position of user waypoints there is an alternative to using lat/long co-ordinates which is often easier, and that is to enter instead the bearing and distance of the new waypoint from a point in your set's fixed database. For example, suppose that your proposed destination is Redhill and that you will be approaching from the West. It easy enough, of course, to enter the airfield's ICAO code of EGKR, as that will be in your set's database. However, the joining procedure, and common sense, require you to join via the VRP, JUNC M25/M23, and you will be much better prepared for an organised join if you have that in your database (and Route, if you assemble one). Most airfield guides show the lat/long co-ordinates of VRPs and you can always enter those in your User Waypoint list. Some guides also give VOR/DME co-ordinates as well. For example, the M25/M23 junction may also be shown as BIG 240deg 7.2nm. Even it is not, it is easy enough, from your armchair and using only the compass rose over BIG on the map and a navigational scale, to discern that this VRP is around 240 deg from BIG and about 7 miles. That is quite accurate enough for your purposes. Entering REF: BIG. BRG: 240. DST: 7.0 nm is much easier and less subject to error than entering N5115820 W00007620 and then checking that you have got it absolutely right.

Naming User Waypoints is a tricky matter. It is very easy to forget what you might have called a waypoint if you find yourself trying to find it in your list some months or years later. There is no ideal answer but whatever method you use, you must always be consistent. Six digits is about as much space as most sets will allow you and personally I have found that just entering the first six digits works best. Once you start trying to abbreviate names, unless you have some cast iron and invariable rules of abbreviation, you will find yourself wondering whether you entered REIGATE RAILWAY STATION as RGTRST, RGTRYS REIGRS or whatever. I just take the first six digits of the name, with no attempt at abbreviation, so I would use REIGAT. That works fine until you run up against two waypoints with the same first six digits: there is no obvious solution, but the essential is always to be consistent in your method.

The most popular function of a Satnav set is the GoTo or DIR button. Press that and enter the next desired waypoint and you will be presented instantly with something like: BRG (i.e. Required Track), DST (Distance), TRK (track currently being flown) SPD (Ground Speed currently being flown) and ETE (time that it will take you to reach the waypoint, at current ground speed). Compared with the difficulties of traditional visual navigation methods, this is simply magical and it is no wonder that most VFR pilots these days use Satnav as their primary method of navigation. What they should also do is to check their progress against some other navigational system and if they do not they will, sooner or later, come badly unstuck.

There are numerous ways of coming unstuck with Satnav and by far the most common is making a mistake when inputting co-ordinates. Gross errors are usually detected early but small errors are the most insidious and dangerous.

The next most common Satnav problem is failure of the set. If battery driven, it may run out of power and even if you carry spares, changing batteries and flying the aircraft at the same time can be fraught with risk. Even when there are no problems at your end, however, there can be insufficient satellites in a useable part of the sky to provide an accurate plot.

You will at least know when your batteries are flat or there is insufficient satellite coverage, but what is far more dangerous is the partial failure of the satellite system itself, which leads to your set acquiring a mistaken idea of where you are. If you have paid many thousands of pounds for an IFR set fitted with Receiver Autonomous Integrity Monitoring (RAIM) then it may (or sometimes may not) tell you that there is a problem. Most sets, however, do not have RAIM and therefore you will have no way of knowing about the false position reporting unless you are continually running a check of your navigational progress using some alternative navigational system. For VFR pilots this will usually be the traditional navigational method but you might alternatively use, for instance, VOR/DME.

Safety Sense Leaflet No 25, as described above, sets out in some chilling detail the possible errors to which Satnav is heir to. There are, in fact, 12 or these and in many cases the operator will have no way of knowing when any of these are affecting the accuracy of the set. So this is why it is so essential continually to run a check against what your Satnav set is telling you. For nearly all of the time you will find that your set is spot on, and because of this there are some who have convinced themselves that 'nearly always' must mean for practical purposes, 'absolutely always'. If you have become one such, there is probably nothing that I can say that will convince you otherwise and the realisation of the error of your ways will have to wait until the day arrives when, despite your having put in fresh batteries and double checked the accuracy of all your entries, your set takes you somewhere that you had not intended to go. Let's hope that this does not prove to be overhead Heathrow.

To use 'first generation' Satnav reliably, therefore, you have to invest serious effort at the flight planning stage. In addition to all the work required for planning a route using traditional visual navigation methods, you will have also to enter into your User Waypoint list any new waypoints not in the database and you may also choose to compile a Route in your set. Choose your route to suit the visual navigation method rather than stringing together a route made up of airfields and navigation beacons that are already in your database. You will find that a route made up from airfields and navigation beacons is usually difficult to fly visually and may include waypoints that are difficult to identify or legs that are difficult to follow. As with any well chosen visual navigation routes, choose line features to follow where you can. Motorways are usually easy to follow and their junctions often make good waypoints.

If you are going to use radio navigation as your alternative system, and this is useful if you choose VORs as your waypoints, then you will need to plan accordingly.

Whatever alternative system you choose, it will have to be planned for and you will have to add to your preparations the entering of any waypoints whose co-ordinates are not already in your database. Draw your tracks on your map and enter their details on your flight log. Then enter the waypoint names and co-ordinates and if you have a portable Satnav set, enter these in the set if they are not already within it and the Route as well if you choose. If you cannot access the set until just before the flight then allow sufficient extra time for these extra chores. They must not be rushed. Be sure to add in any extra waypoints that may come in useful, allowing, for instance, for a diversion around a CTA should the controller deny a crossing clearance.

You need to appreciate that because your alternative navigation system – visual, radio or whatever – is more difficult to operate than Satnav, you must plan for it properly so that you can use it with relative ease to monitor your progress against the commands of the Satnav set. Should Satnav appear to be in conflict with your alternative you can then easily check your alternative navigation and if convinced that it is correct you will be able to continue with it without any great difficulty. It is a great mistake to choose your route simply by using whatever waypoints are in your database and then hope to be able to monitor progress accurately and simply and to be able to continue without the benefit of Satnav if that need should arise. Using airfields as waypoints simply because their codes are in the database can be a particularly foolish approach. Although this is quickly set up on the Satnav set, the route may well take you through the ATZs of successive airfields. Such a route will be fraught with high risk unless you are going to be flying a good deal more than 2,000 ft AGL and therefore above the ATZs. Even then you will need to be in radio contact with each airfield well before you reach its overhead. So more work at flight preparation stage will lead, as is so often the case, to less work in the air. A route based on waypoints that suit your alternative system may well take longer to plan for, but will be easier and safer in the air.

Most Satnav sets have a Route or Flight Plan facility whereby you can enter a whole route and also save it for re-use in the future. Of course, it takes longer to enter a whole route rather than just checking that all the waypoints on a proposed route are in the database. In the air this facility provides the advantage of having each leg already entered in advance as opposed to having to enter GoTo or Dir for successive waypoints as each previous waypoint is reached. There is a further advantage at the flight planning stage, however. As you enter in your Satnav set each leg of your proposed route while flight planning you can check the track and distance shown by the set against your planning log for your alternative system. If they prove not to be in agreement then there must be a mistake somewhere which you can then resolve at the flight planning stage rather than facing a navigational crisis subsequently while flying the route.

Second Generation Satnav

So far as flight planning is concerned, the practice used for older sets should be applied in the same way with a second generation set. It is when airborne that the more user friendly resources of the newer equipment shine forth. There are two particular areas where the set offers appreciably greater value and these are easier checking against visual navigation and easier diversion via an unplanned waypoint.

Checking against visual navigation is easier simply because your position is marked for you on what comes close to a conventional 1:500,000 topo map. While a first generation set will tell the pilot that they are so many degrees or cross track nautical miles off track and so many nautical miles from the next waypoint, this information will require time and effort from the pilot to turn it into a position on the map. The pilot may be distracted by some other task or may simply be disinclined to bother with the extra chore but either way, this task may be left undone and the navigation may become degraded to a process whereby the Satnav set's instructions are followed blindly without any real check. Having your Satnav derived position marked clearly on your topo map equivalent makes checking your Satnav position against the terrain so much less demanding and therefore so much more likely to be carried out.

If you ever have to divert from your planned route, perhaps to avoid weather or through lack of a clearance, the second generation set really comes into its own. Move the cursor to the desired next waypoint and press GoTo or Dir and the new track line and all the navigational figures will be immediately presented. With an 'old' set, given the impossibility of safely entering new waypoint co-ordinates while flying, diversions present considerable problems. Before very long we shall all be flying VFR with large and detailed moving maps and the problems that had to be faced with first generation sets will be a matter for fond reminiscence only. We shall, however, continue for some time to have to live with the same residual unreliability of Satnav that we do today and so shall still need to run some other navigation system simultaneously as a check.

A Skymap IIIC

Preparation

Preparation

The aerial-voyage experience has three phases: the preparation, the voyage itself and what used to be called the debriefing until political correctness required that this innocent word be expunged from decent society. "Post-flight assessment" is probably acceptable, and why use one word when three will do instead?

As a useful rule of thumb, the preparation for a flight to somewhere new should take at least as long as the flight itself. During your PPL training you were probably encouraged to come into the school some considerable time before take-off so that you could do your preparation while being supervised. The weather, the airfield information, NOTAMs and pre-flight information bulletins and any other information needed was to hand either in the school itself or at the airfield flight-briefing room. Those facilities are most likely still available to you unless you are now operating from a private strip, but in any case you may find it more convenient to do some at least of your preparation at home or at your workplace. For this you will need an up to date flight guide and access to weather and NOTAM information. Weather information can be obtained fairly easily in a variety of ways – see the latest issue of GET MET for details. While most of this is obtainable in an easily understood format a particular area of difficulty is the language used for TAFs and METARs. No doubt you studied the Met abbreviations for your PPL but unless you regularly consider TAFs and METARs your memory of the host of abbreviations used and even of the format conventions will be hazy. Can you recall, for example, what BLW or LSQ signify? A full list of abbreviations and a description of the format can be found on www.metoffice.com/aviation but people often run out of time and energy and just guess. While I appreciate that this information has to be presented in this obscure form to meet ICAO conventions dating back to the days of Telex I cannot understand why the same information is not presented also in plain English so that leisure aviators can be as well informed as are their professional colleagues. Meanwhile you must do what you can to cope with this inaccessible presentation and the one possible confusion that you must always guard against, especially if you are reading TAFs or METARs on some flying club notice board, is that you are reading today's weather and not yesterday's. The date code appears at the beginning – always check it.

The inaccessibility of Met information is as nothing compared with NOTAMs. The appropriate website is www.ais.org.uk/ As with the Met Office site, you have to register for your first visit and should keep a record of your User Name and Password for future visits. Incidentally, this is also the website for the Air Information Publication (AIP) where you will find, amongst other things, Air Information Circulars. You might have imagined that the AIP would be found on the CAA website, but it is in fact on this National Air Traffic Services provided site. The Home Page of this site will offer you menus into various sources of information and the usual choice when preparing a flight will be Narrow Route Briefing. If you use this page you will have to enter dates, times, ICAO codes of departure and destination airfields and waypoint information if not flying direct. For a VFR flight you should normally enter 'VFR' in the Flight Level box. Alternatively you can just ask for all the information for a given Flight Information Region. You will probably then find yourself looking through several pages, much of it irrelevant to your requirements.

There are also paid for services providing weather, NOTAM and other information for aviators, of which www.avbrief.com is a popular example.

You can still manage without a computer or fax as long as you have a telephone. The weather can be obtained by AirMet, you can book out by phone, you can file a flight plan by post and activate it on the day by phone. Red Arrows display and temporary restrictions information can be obtained by phone (it's even free – 0500 354802) but you will have to visit a flight briefing room to get the latest NOTAMs and pre-flight information bulletins.

Pilots who visit www.ais.org.uk/ only occasionally often find themselves defeated by its complexity and pilots who have access neither to the internet nor to a notice board with NOTAMs displayed sometimes skip this formality and set out in ignorance of what they might encounter. If this should prove to be a flying display or a temporarily prohibited area the consequences could be dire and I do advise against this most strongly. At the very least, you should always make a call to 0500 354802 and should keep in touch by radio with area air traffic controllers throughout your flight so as to keep out of trouble. This is not recommended practice – just a lot better than doing nothing beyond hoping for the best.

You start your preparation by choosing your route, and making the right choice here is all-important. In some cases there is just one obvious route which will become the inevitable choice, but in many cases there are decisions to be made. Terrain, airspace restrictions, navigational facilities and weather all have to be considered.

Terrain

The major factors here are high ground, sparsely inhabited areas and water. Avoid them all by routing around if you can. If you cannot, try to minimise the time spent over such terrain – especially in a VMC-only single-engined aeroplane

Inhospitable terrain – to be avoided if possible

There are terrain features which provide excellent navigational guidance and you should accept their help gratefully. If, for example, you see that a prominent and easily recognisable town lies near the proposed route, alter the route to fly close to it and you will have a valuable waypoint. Follow line features where you can; railways, coastlines and motorways are favourites and large rivers and lines of hills are often very helpful. The essence of choosing the route is to make the most of what is available, and unless you are consciously seeking a difficult navigational exercise you should make the most of any terrain features going. For your PPL navex (and for your CPL Skill Test for that matter) you would be expected to draw a straight line from A to B and fly it, but these are artificial schoolroom environments. In the real world, if a diversion of ten miles from the straight-line route will give you fifty miles of coastline to follow, go for it.

A prominent line feature. A really useful navigational resource

Airspace Restrictions

Some restricted areas have to be routed around, but by no means all. Class A airspace, danger areas, prohibited areas, restricted areas, Aerodrome Traffic Zones, parachute dropping zones, glider and paraglider launching sites and the like are definite no-nos if active. Class D airspace and Military Aerodrome Traffic Zones are seen by some PPLs as places to be avoided as well, but this is a mistake. You need radio to enter such airspace and you have to comply with Air Traffic Control directions, but don't let these requirements put you off.

Some pilots, inexperienced in the way of control areas, become tongue-tied and tremulous on approaching such areas. They bottle out and creep around the edges, sometimes saying not a word to anyone. They hope that if they say nothing they will pass unremarked, but they delude themselves. While the odd sparrow may fall without being noticed on radar, the passage of an aircraft at 500ft or more AGL and within range of most radar heads is going to be observed – and if the aircraft is not in touch with the controller, the controller is going to become concerned. Any air traffic controller responsible for Class D airspace will tell you of the sad cases who appear on the radar screen every summer weekend, tiptoeing

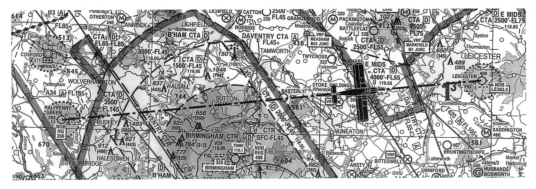

If you want to fly from Wolverhampton Business Airport to Leicester, are you going to tip-toe around the edges of Birmingham CTR, or be a grown-up pilot and fly straight through?

silently around the edges of the area as though they were playing grandmother's footsteps. The routes of such unfortunates are sometimes incredibly complicated as they thread their way through the imagined pitfalls of control areas and MATZs. If they are flying in strange territory they often find following such tortuous paths difficult if not impossible. So all too often they stray into the very airspace which they wanted so desperately to avoid, and end up even more embarrassed than they would have been if they had flown through the airspace with ATC approval in the first place.

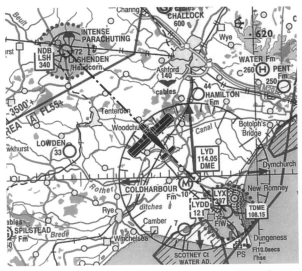

The direct route from Lydd to Lashenden gives little to navigate by as you approach your destination. Why not aim to hit the railway line about five miles to the east and then approach the airfield along the railway?

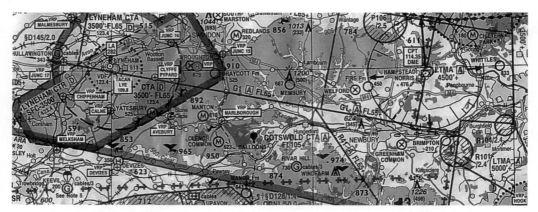

The low level route between the Marlborough Downs and Haydown Hill connects CPT VOR with the Vale of Pewsey, Devizes and beyond. It is clearly marked by the Kennet and Avon Canal and the adjoining railway line

Be bloody, bold and resolute, therefore, and choose a route through Class D's and MATZs. Let's face it – even given that impressive Private Pilot's Licence which you hold, you are not really a *pilot* if you have to creep around the edge of such areas. Chapter 12 tells you how to cope with the Fat Controller without nervous strain for either party.

Having psyched you up to fly straight through such areas, I unfortunately have to warn you that Class D controllers (but not usually MATZ controllers, who are renowned by and large for their helpfulness) will sometimes tell you when you call them for clearance through their area that they are too busy to let you in just now. At the time of writing, Bristol and Luton were areas which tend to regard themselves as fine but rather private places so far as transiting VFR traffic is concerned. It is therefore as well to have in reserve a Plan B for routing around them if you are forced to.

Navigational Facilities

Some routes are easy to fly visually and you may decide that you will need help from no other navigational facilities in any case. However, there are many routes, especially those into unfamiliar surroundings, where radio aids can be very useful. The location of VORs (with or without co-located DMEs), of NDBs and of VDF facilities may therefore have a bearing on your choice of route.

This is so even if you also have Satnav. Unless you have a panel-mounted example and it is classed as having full IFR capability, you can use your Satnav only as a back-up to other navigation techniques. If you would in any case have flown the route by visual navigation alone without Satnav, you need not consider the assistance available from radio aids. But if without Satnav you would have looked for some assistance from radio aids, you should continue to do so. Choose a route in these circumstances therefore which maximises the assistance available from radio aids even if you do possess Satnav.

The Weather

The days when weather does not play a crucial part in aeronautical voyages are unfortunately all too few in Northern Europe. The probability of a longish VFR flight being weathered off must be around one in three in the summer and nearer 50:50 in the winter. You can get one-, two-and three-day look-aheads by fax and on the internet but no forecast is ever 100% reliable and the more distant it is, the less reliable it gets. Cloudbase, visibility and strong winds are the usual issues, but the diversity of problems European weather can throw at us is amazing.

The relative newcomer to route flying will probably be looking for an actual or estimated minimum cloud base of about 2000ft above ground level, and visibility of at least five miles. In time you may decide to reduce these personal minima to something less, particularly when flying over familiar terrain, and a cloudbase of perhaps 1000ft AGL with visibility of 5nm may be judged acceptable by a more experienced VFR pilot.

Whatever your personal minimum cloudbase above surface level may be, you need to have in readiness – if at all possible – a low-level route. This may be the only route which you plan, or it may be an alternative kept up your sleeve in case of low cloudbase. Because low-level visual navigation is more difficult than steaming along in CAVOK at FL40 with several counties laid out beneath you, you need to keep the visual navigation simple. Furthermore, the range of radio navaids apart from Satnav becomes less when you are flying low and there will be much less help from them when you operate at low level – just when you needed them most.

Low-level routes necessarily tend to follow valleys. Fortunately rivers, railway lines and many roads tend to do the same. These are just the sort of line features you need to aid your visual navigation, and your low-level route should make the most of them. The sea offers the lowest terrain going, and a route which hugs the coast is sometimes the best for low-level aviation although sea fog can sometimes spoil this cunning plan.

Maps and Flight Log

With the route or alternative routes selected, you can now fold your maps appropriately and mark them with your route(s). Next comes the weight and balance considerations. In some cases it will be self-evident that you will be within your maximum weight and centre-of-gravity limitations. But if there is any doubt at all, the appropriate calculations have to be made as set out in the POH/FM. During your training, when you were flying all the time with only one or two up and little baggage, you got used to ignoring weight and balance considerations; the SOP (Standard Operating Procedure) was to fill the tanks full and set off. But once you start taking on passengers and their baggage, you have to make these calculations and decide what baggage and fuel limits will be necessary.

Customs and Police

The anti-terrorist regulations require you to give the police 24 hours notice of flights to Ireland, the Isle of Man and the Channel Islands. Notification of British and foreign customs officers can be dealt with at the same time. These notifications are always best given in writing – fax or letter – and copies taken with you.

Finally you can begin the preparation of your flight log. You will be able to enter tracks, distances, nav and com frequencies and much else besides. Headings, speeds, times and fuel-consumption estimates will have to wait until the day itself when you will have the winds and temperatures.

Preparations on the Day

These include:

> Aircraft: is it available and serviceable?

> Weather: are the forecast and actual both within your personal limits for the entire route together with any alternates?

> NOTAMs, Pre-flight Information Bulletins and temporary restrictions: checked out?

> Destination airfield(s): contacted and cleared? Some airfields are 'Prior Permission Required' (PPR) and this usually means calling by telephone before take-off rather than by radio when in flight. However, it never does any harm to telephone an airfield – especially the smaller ones – in any case. Quite often you will receive useful current information about the field which is available neither from the flight guide nor from NOTAMs. It is, for example, far more convenient to learn over the telephone before take-off than it is over the radio when you call for joining instructions that because of last night's rain the airfield is now waterlogged and closed.

> Flight log completed: now that you have the winds and temperatures you can fill in the remaining gaps.

> Booking out or flight plan: done or filed.

By the time you have completed all the above, assembled your passengers, refuelled and done a dozen other last-minute things, you may be wondering as you strap yourself in whether it's ever worth all the effort. Strictly speaking, I fear that the answer may be that in the early stages of your aerial voyaging, it is not. But that is simply because the whole procedure is new to you and everything takes three times as long as it will do once you become more experienced. What tends to take the pleasure out of the business of preparation for flying a route is that time seems to slip through your fingers on the day. So you sometimes find yourself with another hour's work to do before your estimated time of departure which by now is only fifteen minutes away. If you want to enjoy the whole experience rather than end up over-stressed and unhappy, the solution is to allow yourself lots and lots of time for the final preparations. If the upshot is that to give yourself plenty of time for a take-off at 1000 you have to get up at 0500, do that thing. And if, in the event, you find yourself with all preparations completed at 0900, you can either continue your day with an hour in hand – which tends to stress-free living – or you can award yourself a well-deserved second breakfast.

Ready for the off. The Captain has put in a great deal of preparation to get to this stage. And it will all be well worth while

As you get to know the ropes, you will find that you can complete a competent and thorough preparation in far less time than it originally took you. And then, I promise you, there will no longer be any question as to whether it is all worth while.

Coping with the Fat Controller

Coping with the
Fat Controller

Chapter 12

In the Beginning

In the beginning there was the sky. Then there was the pilot; he saw that the sky was good and he thundered across it and revelled in it. Godlike he looked down from it and childlike he cavorted about in it. Later there was the Air Traffic Control Officer (ATCO) and he saw that if the sky was not going to be filled with the noise of much light alloy in collision there were going to have to be some changes made. And so the great days of freedom of the skies were brought to a regrettable close. A new trammelled, curtailed and altogether regulated regime has supplanted those heady days when, if you wanted to fly from Eastbourne to Edinburgh, you got into your aeroplane and you just went. And you went along any route at any height that took your fancy on that particular day. And if you got a bit lost, you flew low over railway stations where the names were obligingly painted on the roof. And if you could not find yourself a railway station, you landed in a field and asked.

Even in the present day, if you fly from an airfield surrounded by uncontrolled airspace and you never leave your local area, you can still carry on in more or less the good old way – although railway stations are much less plentiful than they were, and none have their names on the roof. And popping into some stranger's field to ask the way is now a contravention of the Air Navigation Order. However, you would be a very unadventurous sort of pilot never to leave your local area. And unless you wish to try the difficult, uncertain and often calamitous technique of threading your way about the country avoiding all controlled airspace, you will inevitably find yourself sooner or later exchanging messages across the airwaves with the dreaded Fat Controller.

Most private pilots accept, perhaps reluctantly, the need for Air Traffic Control but find it does nothing to add to the joy of flying and can sometimes ruin their whole day. The low-hour private pilot tends to see the average ATCO as a necessary evil to be endured rather than welcomed. Talking to any strange controller tends to set this pilot's pulse racing in anticipation of being made to look foolish in front of everyone else listening out on the frequency. If the strange controller should be impatient, unhelpful or even downright hostile, the confusion and the shame may know no bounds. Some research in the USA revealed the interesting fact that the stress levels recorded in some student pilots before pressing the transmit button exceeded the amounts generally recorded in military pilots about to enter actual combat. The conclusion is therefore that for some the fear of imminent death is less alarming than the fear of imminent humiliation on the airwaves. As it will be the ATCO who may inflict that humiliation, it is not surprising that some pilots feel somewhat antipathetic to ATCOs.

If this antipathy is less than just to the ATCO, does the latter see the average low-hour PPL in a friendlier light? Alas, no. All too often the private pilot comes across to most ATCOs as depressingly unpredictable and disorganised – and while most can live (albeit reluctantly) with the disorganised state of the low-time PPL, it is their **unpredictability** which really gets them going in the control tower.

From the Control Tower

Look at the situation from Air Traffic's point of view. ATCOs deal with a mix of commercial and private aviation. Commercial aviators usually fly IFR even in VMC. This implies pre-ordained routes with standard arrival and departure patterns. So the controller knows all the time not only where the commercial aircraft is (thanks in many cases to a transponder with Mode C in addition to the fact that a laid-down procedure is being flown) but also what it is going to do next. Knowing where an aeroplane is and what it will be doing shortly is a source of great comfort to a controller, who can sit there sipping the mid-morning hot chocolate with that soothing feeling of having all the beans in a nice little row.

But then there may come within the ambit of that controller's attention some hapless private pilot who wishes to cross the area and would like to talk to someone kind. So far as the ATCO is concerned, anything

A local (tower) controller at work. Not fat at all, actually

may happen now. The initial contact may give no more than a callsign and some vague statement such as "Crossing your area." So first of all the relevant information has to be dragged out of the pilot. Having at last been persuaded to give a present position, quite possibly the said aviator causes immediate confusion by giving one which does not tally with the VDF read-out on his transmission. So our man is not actually where he thinks he is. Possibly he is unable or unwilling to squawk, and in the absence of an adequate radar return the controller cannot be sure where the aircraft is. The only available information is that, according to the VDF, it is currently on a bearing of 065° from the field.

After the consumption of prodigious amounts of airtime, the pilot eventually divulges that his flight is from Barton to Elstree, but he has not been so good as to reveal what his next intended waypoint is. So all the controller has gleaned so far is that the aircraft ought to be progressing in a vaguely south-easterly direction. Bitter experience tells the ATCO that it is quite likely that the pilot will shortly come to realise that his position report was wrong, and may then make a substantial change of heading. Provided that the aircraft is flying under VFR and is outside controlled airspace, it can do whatever it takes a fancy to. But since its position was incorrect, it may easily blunder unintentionally into any controlled airspace that might just get in its way. So from the ATCO's end of the transaction, what he or she now has in the area is a loose cannon which might do anything. Unless the aircraft can definitely be identified on radar, Air Traffic may be unable to save the pilot from his own incompetence. By now the controller's hot chocolate has gone cold, the pulse rate has risen, the adrenalin has begun to flow and a distinct state of antipathy to private pilots (as compared to those nice organised and **predictable** commercial pilots) has set in.

Area (approach) controllers at work. Quite nice people when you get to know them

Caustic Controllers

What we have, then, is PPLs on the one hand fearful of talking to controllers because of the risk of being made to look foolish, and controllers unhappy about private pilots wandering about their area with little idea as to where they are and less idea about what they are going to do next. The great majority of controllers demonstrate saint-like qualities of forbearance, remaining polite and solicitous in the face of tongue-tied confusion on the part of the PPL. For just a few controllers however, it is all too much. In the face of frequent provocation they find that their position of power begins to corrupt, and they can no longer resist the temptation to put the private pilot down.

Judging from the sort of remarks sometimes made over the radio these days, I would venture that a few ATCOs see low-hour PPLs as veritable blots on the skyscape to be humiliated and discouraged at every opportunity. To give examples of the sort of remarks I mean:

To an aircraft receiving a Radar Information Service flying visually one cloudless summer evening, and indeed the only aircraft on frequency:

> *"G-**, have you altered your heading?"*
>
> *"G-**, negative."*
>
> *"G-**, your heading has changed five degrees. Do not alter your heading without informing me."*

To an aircraft that has just volunteered the information that there are two balloons located five miles out on the approach to the runway in use:

> *"G-**, we don't want to know about balloons to the east of the field."*

To an aircraft that has just come on frequency giving position and route reports; the route will take the aircraft five miles from the small airfield and 3,000 ft above it:

"G-**, keep well clear of this airfield and report when changing frequency."

To an aircraft that is about to take off and has called:

"Tower, G-**, check QNH is 1005."

"G-**, if you had made a note when you were given your clearance, you would know it is 1005."

A call at dawn, three minutes after the airfield has officially opened and from the only sign of life anywhere. It is about a mile to the briefing room, which is probably locked at this unearthly hour, and it is raining.

"Tower, G-**, on the south side, can I book out by radio, please."

"G-**, booking out has to be carried out in person at the control-tower briefing room on the telephone link to the control tower. This is so as to save air time."

How about this exchange between an aircraft on an initial Instrument Rating Test:

"**** Approach, Exam **, request the frequency of the DME located on your field."

"G-**, that information is not available. You should refer to the latest editions of Jeppesens or Aerads."

Or this fairly common response from a certain regional airport inside controlled airspace:

"G-**, negative. You are not clear to cross controlled airspace because of traffic." (The "traffic" over the next five minutes amounts to two movements.)

Note that in all these real-life examples the ATCO is within his or her rights but is nonetheless using the opportunity to put the pilot down. The unspoken message is that the pilot is either a wally or a nuisance or both, and that the local airspace would undoubtedly be improved by his or her absence. Such attitudes are evinced by relatively few ATCOs, and as a general rule I would say that you are more likely to encounter it at the occasional regional airport where commercial and private flights use the same airspace. To a small minority of controllers of such airspace, commercial flights are seen as revenue-producing and private flights as nuisance-producing. Controllers at general aviation-only fields are not usually a problem and indeed have been known to volunteer over the radio a taxi or accommodation.

Experienced pilots can no doubt take in their stride the odd frotty controller, and in any case are far less likely to suffer the rough end of the tongue of an irritable ATCO than is the unfortunate tyro. Of much greater concern is the effect that these controllers are likely to have on safety and on flying training. I do not know whether Human Factors is now a compulsory part of the syllabus of ATCOs as it is of pilots, but if it is not, it certainly should be. We have all read of classic accidents caused by members of a crew failing to communicate properly, and how this is often the result of the captain putting down his crew so that they hesitate to relate to him any more than they have to. When an emergency arises there is sometimes just not enough habit of teamwork left to cope with the circumstance, and the result is a tragedy. Likewise, an inexperienced pilot, fearful of yet another put-down at the hands of an antagonistic controller, can very easily shrink from asking for clarification of half-understood instructions. And the extra stress imposed by the controller's sarcasm when the inexperienced pilot is already at the limit of his or her ability may lead to some really foolish decision – or, through inattention to essential aircraft handling requirements, to "loss of control at low level" as the accident reports so often put it.

Where flying training is concerned, unpleasant and authoritarian controllers must put quite a few off training altogether. Such persons are going to be a significant discouragement to any but the least sensitive student, although they are effectively part of the training system. There are of course many stresses in the life of an ATCO and there must always be a temptation to take it out of the tyro pilot because he or she is the easiest target to hand – much the same as kicking the cat. But the more of a pedagogue the ATCO becomes, the more the student will be imbued with the very dangerous concept that the controller is actually in control of the flight. A dictatorial attitude on the part of ATCOs will tend to encourage a dependence on them. This will become a serious disadvantage one day when margins of safety have for some reason reduced to no more than a hair's breadth and the poor misguided pilot is instinctively trying to communicate when his or her only chance of survival lies in aviating and navigating.

Consummate Controllers

Fortunately the vast majority of ATCOs are not monsters and some of the messages they have offered me over the years have been distinctly helpful. Herewith a small selection:

> *"G-CK, on your present heading you will shortly enter the London TMA. I suggest that you descend immediately to 2400ft.*
>
> *"Red 3, check your wheels are down and locked."* (They weren't!)
>
> *"G-TI, hold your position. You seem to have a concrete block tie-down attached to your port wing."* (I wasn't the captain and I hadn't done the external checks – honest!)
>
> *"G-IG, Compton Abbas is now in your 10 o'clock at 1 mile range."* (That was Boscombe Radar speaking – I was getting short of fuel, the cloud base was lowering the rain was getting heavier and they were guiding me through the murk to fuel and safety.)
>
> *"G-IG, while you are clear to take off on 13, it does seem to me that you have actually lined yourself up on 31. As long as you don't mind a downwind take-off, I don't mind you taking off on 31."* (What a gentle let-down in the circumstances, and what a meal some ATCOs would have made of that situation!)

Although I could relate many more examples of the Fat Controller saving the day for me, these examples are perhaps enough to demonstrate that ATCOs can be seriously useful to private pilots. In my view, therefore, the name of the game must be not just to go out there hoping to escape any unpleasantness with Air Traffic, but positively to use their services to help you along your uncertain way. Here is how to do it.

Say Again?

The first thing to do is to make sure that your radio equipment is good enough for you to be able actually to communicate with ATC. If it is not, you are wasting everyone's time. The first aircraft of which I was ever a part-owner had many fine qualities but a poor radio. It had insufficient volume to be adequately audible when the engine (all 68bhp) was at full power, so that in the climb you had to throttle back to use it at all. Even then it was very difficult to make out what was being said, and not much easier for air traffic to hear your transmissions. Indeed it was so bad that we proposed changing its call sign to 'Golf – Say Again'. We tried various measures to improve its performance but these made little difference, and it was only when we eventually agreed to bite the bullet and buy a new set that I realised what a serious handicap a poor radio had been. In the ensuing months we all found ourselves setting out on journeys to further-flung parts than we would have contemplated before with our inadequate radio. The new box gave all of us much more confidence, and since that day I have always insisted where I could on a radio with first-class performance. It makes a massive difference to your dealings with the Fat Controller if you can each understand what the other is saying without strain.

To Err is Errmanlike

Once you have got a decent radio, the next thing is to consider what it is that you propose to say to Their Nibs down there over the now tolerably clear R/T. I referred a little earlier to continuing along your uncertain way, and I used that word "uncertain" advisedly because the VFR pilot who says that he is always certain of his position throughout every flight is either a liar or a master of self-deception. So it is fundamental that you accept that sometimes your conception of your position will be a little vague. Furthermore, you need also to accept that there will often be other features of your operation which turn out less than perfect. You may, for instance, fly right past your destination airfield without identifying it. You may turn the radio volume down momentarily and then forget to turn it up again, so that when you discover your mistake you will be uncertain whether you have missed any calls. You may make a left turn out when you were cleared for a right turn. You may…well, you may do almost any foolish thing.

The reason for your incompetence is simply that you are human, and all humans – without a single exception – are fallible. The culture of flying training seems quite wrongly to imagine a goal where the qualified pilot performs all operations perfectly, and any slippage below perfection is regarded as a regrettable lapse from the required standard. This is, of course, absolute nonsense, and I can assure you that in the world of aviation – just as in all other fields of human endeavour – mistakes are being made by everyone all the time. Admittedly those who are experienced and in good practice are making mistakes less often than the rest, but even they will still cock something up from time to time.

The main purpose of all the drills and checks which pilots perform *ad nauseam* is to overcome mankind's lamentable fallibility and tendency to forget things. Checks and drills go a long way to reduce these failings, but they never eliminate them entirely. That is why the more important matters have to be checked twice or thrice, simply in the hope that the issue will receive proper attention at least once. So when you carry out your pre-flight checks, these will probably include at a very early stage a check to see that the parking brake is on. The engine-starting check will include another parking-brake check before firing up, and, if you were well brought up you will instinctively apply the foot brakes as well before actually turning the starter key. If people were robots, only one brake check would be necessary. But they are not, and it is dangerous nonsense to carry on as if they were.

Accept, therefore, that you will make some mistakes along your route. Although this will be regrettable, it will probably be no big deal and no more than others have done before and will do again. So it is perfectly OK to make the odd mistake. What is even more important is that it is equally OK to admit to the Fat Controller, if the mistake affects him, that you have done so. Indeed, if you fail to admit your mistake you may compound the fault, whereas if you do admit it you will find that most errors will be treated as no more than part of an ordinary day's business. So the cardinal rule is to keep Air Traffic informed all the time of anything which affects them. If you are uncertain about something relevant, don't hesitate to tell them that as well. For example, you think you have flown right past your destination airfield without identifying it. According to your timing it should have passed beneath you a minute ago. Reject the temptation to keep silent while hoping that something will turn up, and boldly come out of the closet and tell the Fat Controller the situation:

> *Tower, G-**, I do not have the airfield in sight although I expected to pass it a minute ago.*

So now ATC knows how you are fixed and becomes part of the loop devoted to finding your way to the airfield. Help from radar or VDF may be available, or the controller may be able to guide you in relation to prominent local landmarks. Even if no material assistance whatsoever can be offered, at least Air Traffic knows what is going on at your end rather than having to speculate. So you are likely to receive more helpful and sympathetic treatment than if you had said nothing, leaving the controller eventually to inquire where you were and what you were doing.

It's the same if you forgot to turn up your radio volume for a while or turned left on the climb-out rather than right. Always tell the Fat Controller if something relevant has gone wrong and you will most probably get him on your side. The essential point is that it is the **unpredictability** of private pilots which irritates controllers. Do tell them what is going on in the cockpit, rather than just hoping that if nothing is said they won't notice poor little you bumbling about up there.

Conversing with Them Indoors

Consider how best to conduct your conversations with the Fat Controller. In a word, your conversational style should be professional. Work out what you are going to say before you say it (operate brain before mouth); write it down first if that helps. Get all the information likely to be wanted into the one call, be brief and sound confident even if you're not very. Don't – I beg of you on bended knee – address the controller as "sir", "ma'am", or use Americanisms such as "at this time". I also have a strong personal prejudice against pilots who refer to themselves as "we", as though they are either a Royal Flight or else leading a formation of Spitfires back from a Rhubarb over Normandy. Indeed, sounding professional does not require you to pretend that you are some world-weary 10,000-hour aviator – just someone who has a fair idea of what they are about.

I do realise that for the beginner, all this is a good deal more difficult than it sounds. After a while off flying I often find myself mentally freezing before the first call of the day, and I can remember the days when every call was agony and every reply seemed totally unintelligible. The best remedy is to get out there and do it. Accept that you are going to make the odd blunder, but keep trying and what seemed impossible will become second nature after a while. Your understanding of reception will be much improved by frequent listening to an air-band receiver. Understanding reception is largely a matter of knowing what the controller is likely to say in any given circumstance. So if you are going to be using, say, a Lower Airspace Radar Service it would be very useful to tune in to one while you are on the ground and work out what is being said.

Once you are able to communicate with ATCOs without difficulty you must examine how to put this skill to your advantage. Most pilots can cope with their local controllers with a little experience, even to the extent of deciding not to start until that miserable swine Blenkinsop goes off-watch at lunchtime. However, if you are continually falling foul of them, some reflection on that state of affairs is desirable. You need to consider whether the unpleasant exchanges are occurring because of your mistakes, their mistakes or misunderstandings between you both. If, for example, you are incurring the displeasure of Them Indoors because of a marked tendency to fly round the circuit in a contrary direction to that specified, or to land on the wrong runway and to take-off without clearance, you really must take steps to put your own house in order rather than blame the tetchy exchanges which ensue on Air Traffic. Even in these circumstances, however, you would have a legitimate complaint if the said controller over-reacts. If he has anything more than a brief comment to make, then the proper time for that is after the flight either face-to-face or over the phone. In these sort of situations it can be quite a good idea for the pilot to take the initiative and say "Tower, G-**, I shall contact you immediately after the flight about this matter."

If the problems are arising partly or wholly because of the conduct of the controllers on your base airfield, you have a problem which needs to be addressed. You really need to explore the position with other local pilots and your local club (if any) before you take any action. Unless you are looking at the very rare case of actual incompetence on the part of the controllers, there is little you can do at an official level. The usual issue is one of unnecessary officiousness towards private pilots, and while there is a whole range of acts of aggravation which might be taken in reply, I would advocate none of these. Instead, I would advise continued attempts to reach an understanding between the controllers and the private pilots. Lines of communication need to be opened and kept open. This is the sort of situation where informal meetings, offers of spare seats on private flights, socialising and so on are more likely to succeed than anything else. But do make sure that the initiative is sustained and not allowed to die away after the first enthusiasm.

If you are going further afield than your local area, you are going to have to talk to strangers. There is a natural inclination for British folk to avoid such conversations, but I do strongly advocate overcoming your reluctance to open your mouth for fear of putting your foot in it and to *get communicating*. On the positive side, you will make the flight safer for yourself and your passengers and you will gain valuable experience. This will make future conversations that much easier – just like speaking a foreign language really. The downside is that you risk making a bit of a fool of yourself if you get things wrong. Well, don't worry too much about that. If you listen to an air-band radio, you may notice that people (even controllers) are getting things wrong all the time. Best of all, I have listened to an unusually unpopular controller at a regional airport whose obsequiousness to airliners was matched only by his scorn for private pilots. Amidst jeers and catcalls, he was unfolding the awful truth to a DC-9 that he had unfortunately directed the pilot up the wrong taxiway; there would not be space to turn unassisted; a tractor was being sent; and the airways slot had been lost...

Write somewhere on your kneeboard a little checklist of the constituents of a request for a Radar Advisory or Information Service, and their proper order:

> Callsign and type
>
> Position
>
> Heading
>
> Altitude or level
>
> Intention (e.g. next reporting/turning point; destination; type of approach; manoeuvring area of levels (band) required etc.)
>
> VFR or IFR
>
> Service required.

This is the sort of information any controller is likely to need on first contact. If he is busy, he may want no more than your callsign to start with. However, you should always have the full range of information at your fingertips when you make contact with a new controller, be it for a radar service or anything else. Don't leave it to him to extract each piece of information from you as though he were a courtroom lawyer trying to quarry out the full facts from a hostile witness.

As with most aspects of flying, it's all about thinking ahead and applying the old grey matter. If you do that and you speak up confidently as the captain in command who knows what he or she is about, you may even find that the dreaded Fat Controller has become actually co-operative and almost human at times!

Low-level
Navigation

Low-level Navigation

Visual navigation at 2000ft or more AGL and at the conventional speed of a light aircraft is a skill fairly easily acquired with practice. But at low level it becomes much more of a challenge. If it is your invariable custom never to fly if the cloudbase is below 2000ft, that is a perfectly valid decision for you as aircraft captain to take. However, even a pilot with such a restrictive personal minimum must accept that sometimes the weather turns out to be somewhat different from expected. So one day there will be no other option for them but to fly lower. Just as a pilot, who is clearly a prudent person, practises forced landings from time to time – hoping for the best but preparing for the worst – so also should low-level navigation be practised as a precautionary measure by all VFR pilots. If the practice is carried out with the cloudbase a good deal higher than the chosen lowest level of operation, there should be no problem in recovering the situation should it get out of hand. You just climb up to an easier height and find out where you went wrong.

The major factor affecting low-level navigation is that your radius of vision is much more restricted than it is higher up. This means that your opportunity to identify a point feature way ahead or abeam, and perhaps navigate in relation to it, is curtailed. Unless they are already familiar to you so that you can identify them immediately on sight, such features appear in front and then disappear behind before you have time to establish what they are. Familiarity is an enormously important factor in recognition from low level. You would probably have no great difficulty in quickly recognising your mother standing in a reasonably crowded market square. Never having had the pleasure of meeting her, I would need a detailed description, with a photograph if possible, and would still take several minutes to pick her out. You, with her image firmly planted in your memory bank, don't have to say to yourself "Medium build, white hair worn up in a bun, blue eyes, that looks like Mum over there". You just know her instantly and instinctively when you see her. Much the same applies to point features and low-level navigation.

As far as practice is concerned, it makes a lot of sense to begin (like Charity) at home. Sooner or later it is likely that you will have to find your way back to your home airfield below a low cloudbase. Being and remaining in good practice at low-level approaches to your base will stand you in very good stead one day. Begin by identifying some easily recognisable features at various points of the compass from your base. The Visual Reference Points around the busier airfields are good subjects for this. Start from your selected feature. If there is a line feature which takes you from your selected start point towards the airfield, use that. If there is a point feature along the way in, route via that feature.

What you are trying to construct is an easily recognisable (and thus easily memorable) route into the airfield. Devise a route for each runway so that you will end up on a downwind or base leg as the airfield comes into sight. With practice you should end up with your personal memory bank loaded with all the low-level routes you are ever likely to need into your field. When you can fly these routes with confidence at 500ft AGL, you are now equipped with approach aids to your airfield which are probably better in many respects than the home-made NDB or Satnav approaches relied on by pilots with IMC ratings for their get-you-home service.

Having mastered the approaches to your airfield, it is now time to extend your low-level navigation skills further afield. By now you will have discovered some important facts about low-level navigation, viz.:

1   There is little time available for looking inside the cockpit.

2   Line features are much more useful than point features.

3   Point features are useful only if you can recognise them more or less instantly.

Any low-level navigation strategy has to be constructed around these factors.

The lack of time available for looking inside the cockpit means that the "office work" has to be kept as simple as possible. A low-level military pilot who does not have the benefits of moving-map and head-up display usually resorts to the construction of a strip map which show just the track and the features on or

The view from 2000ft

The same view from 500ft. At low level many of the visual clues – that coastline for instance – can no longer be seen. You don't get much time to examine those that remain

alongside it. Time notations, fuel states and track changes will be marked, but little if anything else – because simplicity is the keyword. While the construction of strip maps is not vital to the task for the private pilot, it is just as important to grasp the essential notions that you will see only what is on or close to your track; you will be working your way between closely spaced waypoints; and you will rely on elapsed time a good deal for confirmation of position.

You should also realise that you will have little time for setting and adjusting navaids. Many a low-level aviator has become lost while attending to some navaid which was supposed to be helpful but in practice has instead increased the in cockpit workload to an unacceptable level. It is wonderful to be flying along at low level, sure of your position from map, compass, stopwatch and familiarity. It is less wonderful to be flying along fiddling with a navaid, wondering whether you have got it set properly and unsure how to interpret what it is displaying. If you must use it and workload is likely to be a problem, reduce speed, lower a notch or two of flap perhaps and circle some feature while you get the aid properly set up at leisure. Remember the golden rules of low-level manoeuvring; *keep the bank below 45°* and *think airspeed all the time*.

Somebody's mother in a crowd. Not easy to identify – unless you knew her from before

A point feature. Also not easy to identify – unless you knew it from before

The superior utility of the line feature is a godsend for the low-level navigator, and you should never be backward in availing yourself of whatever you can find in this category. If you can track along a railway line, ticking off the towns against elapsed time as you go, happiness and contentment will undoubtedly ensue. Following a nice wide river down to the coast, then following the coast to another river mouth and flying along this toward your destination may be the most intelligent strategy, even if the route is 40% longer than flying direct. You will meet armchair pilots who will scoff at such wimpish practices but you should ignore them. Techniques like these have been long favoured by military low-level operators, and that is surely good enough for the PPL poodling along at about one-fifth of the speed of a marauding fast-jet.

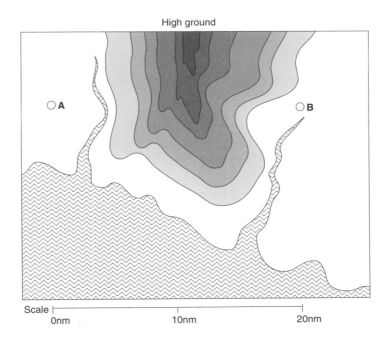

It may be much further to fly by the rivers and coastline, but low level it's probably your best choice

The limited value of the point feature can be greatly improved if it is easily recognised. This may result either from its own special characteristics or your familiarity with it. Another way in which such a feature can be made more recognisable is by use of the stopwatch. If you expect to pass a town three and a half minutes after the last waypoint and indeed you do, it may not be necessary to fly around that town to check its physical features in order to identify it.

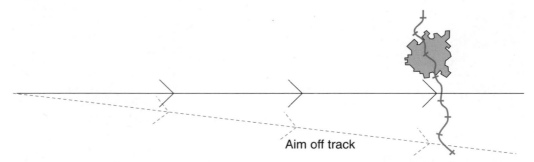

Aim off track

If you reach the railway line but cannot find the waypoint on it you will know that it is somewhere near, either up or down the line. But if you intentionally aim off a bit you will know which way to turn if you cannot see your waypoint

Because of the risk of getting a little off-track and missing a point-feature waypoint, it is necessary to set such waypoints at close intervals – say at about five miles. A departure from track of 10° will put you a bit less than a mile off track after five miles, and the waypoint should still be just within sight from 500ft AGL unless high ground intervenes.

If you can choose a point-feature waypoint which is on a line feature lying across your track, you will make life a lot easier. If you hit the line feature but miss the waypoint, travel up and down the line feature until you have either found the waypoint or at least located yourself on the feature.

But whatever you may do to enhance the identifiability of a point feature, you will never circumvent one awkward fact. Without the aid of a line feature, you will always risk flying past your point without ever seeing it – because you were just far enough off track for it be beyond your limited range of vision.

Alas, there will be times when you are flying over fairly featureless terrain without benefit of line feature towards the next waypoint, which happens to be a potentially easily missed point feature. You will then have to fly a compass heading and rely on accurate track-keeping and elapsed time to find that waypoint. The need for good track keeping should not lead you into the sin of following the HI or compass. The invariable VFR practice of lining up on the instrument and then choosing an outside reference to steer by is more important than ever. By all means check against the HI more frequently, but do not fly by it.

Procedure when Lost

The same principles apply here as apply to navigation at higher levels. However, having established your area of uncertainty, you will probably do better if you can to fly a line feature instead of the usual procedure of flying a fixed heading.

You will of course want to climb as high as possible so as to enlarge your radius of vision, but you should take care not to find yourself amongst broken or scattered cloud. Possibly you have enough instrument-flying ability to enter a cloud and remain in it until you emerge the other side, but this is not the main issue here. It is *crucial* to recognise that at low level the cloudbase is probably well below Minimum Safety Altitude. According to the latest statistics, flight in IMC into the surface accounts for around 20% of all fatalities. Far too frequently pilots fly into "a bit of broken cloud" but never emerge on the other side because of the intervening high ground which had drawn that cloud around it. So it is very important to stay beneath the lowest cloud base, even if that means accepting a limited radius of vision. After all, it is nice to see where you are going all the time, even if you are lost. It is definitely not nice to glimpse the surface occasionally through clouds, any one of which could be stuffed with hill.

It can be helpful at a time like this to slow down and possibly use some flap, which will reduce your stalling speed and give you a better view forward. The ground will now pass below you more slowly and you will be better able to inspect it. If you need more time to examine some surface feature, circle it – taking care to watch angle of bank and airspeed as you do so.

If you decide to call a radar service or Distress and Diversion, be sure to explain that you are a VFR-only pilot and you are limited by the cloudbase of whatever it may be. Otherwise they are very likely to ask you to climb to a better height for radio and radar service.

Marginal VFR weather

By far the best way to handle marginal VFR is to avoid it like the plague in the first place. This means that if you find you are flying into conditions which seem likely to be less than your personal minima, turn round and fly away from those conditions. Make this decision early and you will avoid letting an uncertain situation turn into something worse. If the weather is worsening all around you, divert if you can to the nearest airfield. The Emergency function on a Satnav could come in handy here.

Failing that, a precautionary landing must be considered. Once again, an early decision here will be far preferable to succumbing to the inevitable at the last possible moment. Keep cool, think through each action and take your time in choosing and inspecting your landing site. Provided that you keep control of your aircraft all the way to touch-down and beyond, you and your passengers are unlikely to suffer serious injury. However, if you lose control at any time by stalling, the outcome may be different. The first calls on your attention therefore must always be angle of bank and airspeed.

As you still have power available, you should have the opportunity to inspect your proposed site and reject it if unsatisfactory. However, leaving the decision too late may mean that there is not enough airspace between the surface, the cloudbase and possibly some nearby high ground to leave you the ability to circle and inspect. So the precautionary landing carried out in good time is going to be a whole lot safer than the precautionary landing left to the last minute. Provided that you touch down on a reasonably smooth surface, more or less into wind and at normal speed, all will be reasonably well. If in addition there is enough room to pull up without hitting anything, all will be very well indeed.

I will confess to having left things far too late on an occasion in a motor glider routing from Bristol to Biggin Hill. The forecast was within my personal minima although there was a possibility of snowstorms in the south-east. Following the M25 I flew into one of these just past Reigate. The cloud base was about 1000ft AGL and I had imagined that any reduction in visibility would be acceptable. It was not. To see the ground at all I had to descend to about 250ft, and even then my forward visibility was only about a field and a half. Having decided in principle to make a precautionary landing as soon as a suitable site presented itself, I soon realised that in this restricted visibility there was no chance of circling and inspecting a likely field. If I was going to land, it would have to be from a straight-in approach to a field whose surface would be unknown until the last moment.

I was still following the M25; I knew where I was and the motorway signs were easy to read at this height, giving me a constant update on my position. I knew that there was no high ground on track as long as I stuck to the motorway. I was flying into a strong headwind and had already reduced airspeed, so that by now my groundspeed was less than most of the traffic on the motorway beneath. I therefore elected to stay airborne provided that the visibility got no worse. Turning around was rejected because a straight-in approach and landing downwind would be much more perilous. Eventually the snowstorm passed and I emerged somewhere near Sevenoaks, a good deal older and wiser. Biggin were a bit surprised to hear that I was approaching from the east *en route* from Bristol. If the visibility had got worse, I should have had to land and would risked touching down on bad ground and then turning over. But provided I kept control of the aircraft, I should have been unlikely to suffer serious personal injury – even if I had been the cause of writing off £60,000 worth of aeroplane. It was only good luck which saved me from a serious error of judgement about the acceptability of snowstorms, and since then I have given them a wide berth.

Every VFR pilot risks getting caught out by weather sooner or later. If both pilot and aircraft have good IFR capability, the only way is up – as expeditiously as possible to Minimum Safety Altitude, and down again only in regained VMC or from an instrument approach. *The VFR pilot does not have this option.* If every flying strategy should always offer an alternative way out, as indeed it should, the last option for the VFR pilot is the precautionary landing. It is therefore very much in the best interests of such a pilot to be well versed in low-level low-speed manoeuvring. So keep practising your scales and acquire some experience in farm-strip flying and the precautionary landing will be well within your capability.

VFR into IMC

VFR into IMC

The rule is perfectly simple – VFR-only pilots stay out of cloud. The practice, however, is inevitably more complicated than that. While a few adventurous souls may have a peek inside a cloud just to see what it looks like in there, I doubt that many VFR-only pilots enter cloud intentionally on a regular basis. The JAA PPL syllabus includes four hours of basic instrument flying training but the NPPL syllabus does not. There is some logic in all this if you accept that a JAA PPL is likely to be flying a faster, heavier and lower drag aircraft than a NPPL holder and a crash in IMC is more likely to be fatal in a faster machine. Furthermore, a JAA PPL tends to carry more passengers than a NPPL.

By far the best way to handle the VFR into IMC problem is never to get into IMC in the first place. If you ever should do so, unless you hold at least a current IMC Rating, you are above Minimum Safety Altitude (MSA) and are flying an instrument equipped aeroplane, you will have put yourself seriously at risk and you will not be safe again until you are back in VMC with your aircraft properly under control. However, in the UK it is all too easy for a VFR-only pilot to find themselves inadvertently surrounded by cloud and it is important for every VFR pilot to have a practised strategy for dealing with this frightening and dangerous situation. The situation is dangerous for two distinct reasons:

The hill stuffed with cloud

The classic VFR into IMC accident starts with the pilot scud running in marginal VMC. Suddenly the pilot becomes enveloped in cloud and this can be because of a lowering cloud base, failure to see a cloud ahead or cloud forming around the aircraft, as cloud can easily do in marginal VFR. In such conditions cloud often forms around hills first and finding yourself suddenly enveloped in cloud can well indicate the proximity of high ground. That is not an attractive situation to be in. It is easy to say that the pilot needs to turn away from the high ground and regain VMC but a whole lot more difficult to do with any certainty. If your navigation is spot on you may know where the high ground is and thus know which way to turn to avoid it. That turn may also get you back into VMC as you fly away from the high ground where the cloud tends to form. However, you may not know where the high ground is, or if you did beforehand, finding yourself suddenly in cloud may confuse you so that you lose your sense of where it is. So there you are, enveloped in cloud and uncertain what to do next. If you were scud running and are now below nearby high terrain and obstructions, you are in very serious trouble. I cannot offer any guaranteed remedy and all I can advise is that in such circumstances my own instinct would be immediately to turn, reduce speed and descend gently. If you regain VMC before you hit anything you will count yourself lucky and if not – not. One way out for the scud runner that I should not recommend is to press on, straight and level, hoping to emerge on the other side of the cloud.

If, in spite of its obvious dangers, and, if taken to extremes, its illegality, you will persist in scud running I do advocate staying well below the cloud base. You will soon discover that it is visibility rather than cloud base that is the greater safety determinant and leaving two hundred feet or so between you and the cloud base above is likely to improve the visibility and reduce the chance of inadvertently entering cloud. Reduce speed, lower some flaps, make a precautionary landing or find the safest route back to better conditions and promise yourself never to get into such a fix again.

VFR into IMC scud running accidents seem to occur far more frequently up in the hills rather than down in the plains, and when contemplating a flight over, say, Wales as opposed to, say, East Anglia, you should be far more wary of low cloud bases and other weather hazards. Sudden changes in weather conditions, rapidly forming hill clouds, turbulence, curl over and valleys with no way out and no room to turn are just some of the perils of the hill country. It is best flown over only in settled benign weather and even then you should watch out constantly for changing conditions.

Loss of Control in IMC

It is also possible for the VFR-only pilot inadvertently to enter IMC at something higher than maximum local terrain or obstruction height. If this occurs above MSA, which is 1,000 ft above the highest terrain or obstruction within 5nm, then that would be regarded as sufficient height for safe instrument flying. A quick way of discovering what is likely to be the highest terrain or obstruction in the neighbourhood is to look at a CAA half million topo map for the Maximum Elevation Figure (MEF) appropriate to your position. The MEF is shown as something like 1⁴ representing one thousand four hundred feet and if you add one thousand feet to the MEF you will have a workable MSA. Thus inspection of the map shows that the MSA for the area around Wellesbourne Mountford, to the South of Birmingham is 2,400 ft. Flying safely in IMC above MSA will depend upon the pilot's ability to cope with flying in cloud and maintaining a height above MSA until VMC is regained. The more training and practice in instrument flying that the pilot has undergone, the better will they be able to cope. Loss of control in IMC will be the immediate risk here, leading either to an involuntary spin, or, more dangerously, to a spiral dive at ever increasing speed while the pilot, not recognising the condition, pulls back frantically on the controls, tightening the spiral and eventually causing the break up of the aircraft if it does not hit the ground first.

My belief is that every VFR pilot should have a practised strategy for coping with inadvertent penetration of IMC above MSA. Inadvertent entry into IMC is a serious risk for all VFR pilots and it is very important to think through in advance just what you would do if suddenly presented with this emergency. Formal training and practice in instrument flying is the only safe preventative of loss of control but those who lack either the training or an appropriately equipped aircraft still need to plan how they would cope. In such conditions, the slower and more 'draggy' the aircraft, the greater the chances of survival and microlight pilots seem to survive IMC crashes into hillsides more readily than do aeroplane pilots and passengers.

A level 180 degrees turn by reference only to whatever instruments available should be practised. Most simple fixed wing aircraft are sufficiently stable to look after their pilots for the minute that this will take, provided that the pilot makes no extreme control inputs and ignores 'seat of the pants' sensations. Familiarity with whatever instruments that you have and some practice in using them in simulated IMC are too valuable a safety resource to ignore.

I offer these few tips for the insufficiently trained or equipped instrument pilot who gets caught in IMC:

Many simple aircraft will look after themselves reasonably safely with no control inputs. Even if they do not maintain heading or height, their departure from these may well be quite gradual. Take your aircraft up to a good height in VMC, set it up in the cruise, let go of the controls and see what ensues. Your aircraft may be better able to look after itself on its own rather than with you trying to control it in cloud. If it settles down to a stable descending turn with no input from yourself then, presuming that you know the cloud base to be comfortably above the terrain, your best strategy in such conditions might well be to just let go, and wait until you emerge in your stable descending turn below the cloud base.

Make all your control inputs small and gentle. Over controlling in IMC is all too easy, so if things seem to be getting out of hand, it may well be best to just let go of the controls temporarily.

If all you have is a magnetic compass, then, all other things being equal, flying a Southerly heading makes the compass easier to follow and to hold a constant direction.

If you are using Satnav, the Track indication may provide a direction indicator that is easier to follow than a magnetic compass.

If you want to fly level, set your engine to normal cruise and your trimmer to its usual cruise setting. You are likely more or less to maintain height without any pitch input from yourself. Small pitch adjustments may be better made by small alterations of trim or throttle setting. If you can get your aircraft to fly more or less level with only occasional trim or throttle inputs from yourself, then you can concentrate on the more difficult task of maintaining a heading.

If you want to climb, first turn on to any heading required (probably away from any high ground if below MSA) and then apply the usual engine and trim settings for the climb and try to let the aircraft find its own pitch setting while you gently maintain the approximate heading. Do not attempt to turn and climb at the same time because that is the most difficult handling challenge of all.

If you find yourself in a dive at increasing speed, do not pull back forcefully on the controls as you are probably in a spiral dive and pulling back will simply tighten the turn. Throttle back, correct the turn by banking gently and when you are no longer turning you can ease gently out of the dive. As soon as your speed starts to decrease at all, open the throttle to cruise revs again and trim for the cruise. Concentrate on gently holding your heading and allow the aircraft to settle more or less level.

If you have carb heat, set it permanently ON while in cloud.

If there is an autopilot and you know how to use it, do so. Autopilots are good at instrument flying.

If you have retractable undercarriage, lower it so as to increase drag and decrease the risk of speed building up rapidly in a dive. Adjust power and trim appropriately.

Go up and practise these measures at a safe height in VMC and work out in simulated IMC what will be your best emergency strategy for coping with inadvertent real IMC. As the saying goes: "Hope for the best but prepare for the worst."

Go or No Go

Go or No Go

There are black conditions, when the weather is so dire that cancellation is inevitable. And there are white conditions, when the weather is unquestionably acceptable. And then there are the grey conditions, when you agonise and check the met again and agonise some more, knowing all the time that whatever you decide you will wish you had decided otherwise. We all know the advantage of being down here as compared with being up there on such occasions and fully appreciate the importance of prudence in making the decision. But by the time you have got your PPL, you will be well aware of the fact that VFR flights are cancelled all too frequently in Britain – and usually for very good reason.

The first step in handling the often difficult 'Go or No Go' decision is to acquire the appropriate mindset. This consists of a stoic acceptance that when it comes to VFR flights from A to B in the UK, only about two-thirds will prove possible in summer and perhaps half in winter. So although you have booked the aircraft, organised the passengers, made arrangements at the other end, checked the NOTAMs, done your flight planning and so on, you may still have to throw the whole lot away. Your passengers and maybe your friends at the destination are going to be disappointed, and you will inevitably feel that somehow you have let them all down. Some may suggest or imply that a more competent or courageous pilot would – like the Pony Express – have got through. You will soon learn that these are the same passengers who will be asking to be let out after five minutes aloft. If passengers or others are going to be involved, it is important to make it abundantly clear right from the outset that the whole operation is weather-dependent. That way the loss-of-face factor will be minimised if you eventually have to cancel. It is often useful to have an alternative road, boat or train plan available in case you should have to cancel, because in that way the pressure to say "Go" is less.

Anything else you can do to reduce external pressures on the decision should be put in place. But in the end, with grey conditions prevailing, you are going to have make up your mind and you badly need a reliable method of arriving at the correct decision.

While you were a student pilot, such decisions were made for you. And if you are now renting a club aircraft, your flight will still have to be authorised. The authorisation will probably depend on the application of the club's Flying Order Book, which will set out minimum flight conditions for different levels of experience. In practice the club authorisation system tends to break down in the case of the renting pilot taking-off from an airfield other than base. Such pilots tend to become entirely self-authorising at these times.

At the other end of the spectrum, commercial pilots have to comply rigorously with company rules as to minimum weather conditions. They may reliably expect the company's Chief Pilot to be wanting a word if compliance does not take place, even though the flight at below minima went off without incident. Indeed, if an instrument-rated pilot even *attempts* the final part of an instrument approach with the visibility below the specified minima, the CAA will take an interest regardless of whether the pilot flies for a company or not.

Between the controls and supervision exercised over student pilots on the one hand and commercial pilots on the other, there is a small unsupervised territory occupied by the private self-authorising pilot. It should be no great surprise to learn that this is where we meet the majority of cases of "controlled flight into terrain". Self-authorisation is permitted for these pilots, not because the authorities wish to extend the freedom of the skies on a particularly deserving and responsible group of aviators but simply because there is no practical way of achieving an independent authorising system. Self-authorising pilots are therefore uniquely privileged and also uniquely vulnerable to external pressures and/or lack of experience leading to dangerous decisions.

In the absence of anything imposed upon the self-authorising aviator, it is vital that the PPL decides first to draw up a personal "Company Rule Book" and then to adhere rigidly to it. Without such a regime, the pilot will tend to look first at the weather conditions and then make a decision as to whether they are acceptable. This decision can be dangerously influenced by external factors which have nothing to do with keeping risk at a sensible level. If, on the other hand, that pilot has already decided what their current VFR minima are, the decision is already made – just as it is for the company pilot. Rather than having to agonise over forecasts and actuals, the pilot simply has to ask: "Are the actual or forecast conditions at or above my personal minima?" If they are, then the decision is "Go", and if either are not then the answer is, "No Go".

So how do you arrive at your personal minima? Reading your local club's Flying Order Book would be a good start, and discussing the issue with other more experienced pilots would be helpful. All sorts of factors can be relevant, but the principal ones are probably:

Experience and Ratings

Familiarity with terrain

Recency

Navigational aids

Aircraft type

A good framework to work within is the GAFOR (General Aviation Flight Forecast) notation. This was once in use for British pre-recorded telephone forecasts and is still in use in parts of Europe. It goes as follows:

Oscar	Cloudbase – 2000ft + Visibility – 8000m +
Delta	Cloudbase – 1000ft + Visibility – 3000m +
Mike	Cloudbase – 500ft + Visibility – 15,000m +
X-ray	Cloudbase – less than 500 ft Visibility – less than 1500 m

If either the cloudbase or the visibility falls to less than the appropriate minimum, you move to the lower class. So if the visibility is over 10km but the cloudbase is 1800ft, you are in Delta and not Oscar. Cloudbase is of course in terms of height above the terrain. If the forecast is for Overcast, base 2000ft and you are going to be flying over terrain up to 1200ft AMSL, the base for the purposes of this exercise is 800ft. The base is of cloud which is Broken or Overcast; you can ignore Scattered or Few clouds with a lower base because it is presumed that you will be able to find your way around them.

You can refine these rather broad definitions further if you want to. The French have created subdivisions based on different cloudbases within the same visibility bands of Delta and Mike as follows:

	VISIBILITY			
Cloud Base **(Bkn or O/C)**	**Up to** **1.5km**	**1.5km** **to 3km**	**3km** **to 8km**	**Over** **8km**
Over 2000ft	X	M3	D2	O
1000ft to 2000ft	X	M4	D3	D1
500ft to 1000ft	X	M5	M2	M1

Incidentally, this table illustrates the important point that it is poor visibility rather than low cloudbase which is the more critical factor. The minimum visibility for legal VMC is 1500m at speeds below 140kts. But just try flying VFR with the visibility as poor as this, especially over unfamiliar terrain, and you will soon realise how important visibility is.

Armed with this framework and some due thought and discussion, you can fix your limits. You might decide that for this summer, flying your usual aircraft and while current, your personal minima are perhaps D3 in the local flying area and D1 elsewhere. Subsequent experience, a change in skills or other factors may lead you to modify your minima later in your career.

There can, of course, be further factors to be considered in addition to visibility and cloudbase. For instance, it might be CAVOK but the surface wind is gusting to an unacceptable level. Or the crosswind may be beyond limits; or you may not fancy an hour or two of severe turbulence; or the outlook may be discouraging for the return flight. All these further factors will have to be considered as well. That said, it is cloudbase and visibility which are usually the main determinants.

Having set your minima you must apply them rigorously. No ifs or buts, no exceptions because it looks such a promising day from your bathroom window. If either the forecast or the actual is below your minima, there's no room for debate – it's No Go.

"No exceptions because it looks such a promising day from your bathroom window."

A Typical Flight

A Typical Flight

This is an account of a VFR flight one Saturday in May in which I flew a Piper PA28-200R Arrow from Exeter in the south-west of England to Stapleford, just north-east of London. I offer it, warts and all, as an unexceptional example of how I usually go places when flying VFR. The aircraft had a standard instrument fit with no Satnav. Although pilot and aircraft had IFR capability, Stapleford did not. So IFR was not an option if I was to make it to my destination. It was an option, however, if a diversion should become necessary.

Preparation

Choosing the route

The three-day advanced weather forecast indicated a likelihood of good visibility, moderate winds but possible low cloud. This therefore called for a low-level route. From Exeter to the London area you must first choose whether to go north or south of the Salisbury Plain Danger Area. Because of the useful line-feature coastline from Sidmouth to Poole, I chose to go south on the assumption that the Danger Area at Portland would be inactive.

There are alternative VFR routes out of Exeter in this direction. One follows the old Southern Railway line which passes just north of the airfield. This will take you via Honiton to Axbridge and beyond that to Salisbury, although at only ten miles out from Exeter you come to a potential problem. This is the high ground rising to 800ft just east of Honiton, when the railway goes through a tunnel, and a radio mast rising to 1525ft stands close to the track at this point. So to use this part of the route you need a cloudbase of at least 1300ft AMSL to clear the high ground, and at least 3000m of visibility to enable you to identify and avoid the mast.

However, there is a diversion around the high ground near Honiton. This involves a detour south-east from the airfield on departure until you pick up the coast around Sidmouth. You follow the coast for about 5nm as far as Seaton and then follow the river Axe to Axminster.

Beyond Salisbury you come close both to Boscombe Down MATZ and the Solent Control Area. Boscombe Down is likely to be closed at the weekend, although you can never be sure, but Solent will certainly be in business. There was no need to enter the Solent area but my track would take me close to

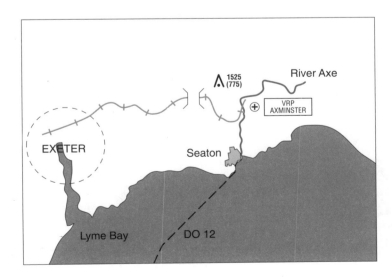

Low level routes from Exeter to the east. Either along the railway or via the coast and up the River Axe

No chance of following the railway line through the tunnel, and going over the ridge will not be possible in low cloud, especially with Honiton Mast beyond

the boundary. The strategy would therefore be to get a radar service from Solent while skirting their area. In this way I would not surprise them at any time and they would keep an eye on me during a tricky stage

Honiton Mast. The main reason why going over the tunnel may not be a good idea

of the route. If I could have been sure of Boscombe being open I could alternatively have opted for crossing their MATZ, although Danger Area 127 might have been an obstacle if it was active at the time.

I chose as a turning point the confluence of the River Test with its tributary from the west, some 3nm north-west of Romsey. Rivers can often prove difficult to identify from the air if they are small and lined with trees along the bank. But I knew from past experience that these particular watercourses are easily seen, and the tributary lies conveniently alongside the railway line from Salisbury to Romsey. I chose as my next waypoint after that the large service station at Sutton Scotney. It lies just south of the intersection of two dual carriageways, the A34 and the A303, and is easy to find and identify. The track between these two waypoints would take me between the Boscombe MATZ and the Solent CTA, except that I would just clip the stub of the MATZ. I could fly beneath the stub by keeping below 1500ft above Boscombe's airfield level of 407ft. I would still, however, be flying too close to the airfield of Chilbolton on the direct route and would have to avoid this. In practice, I would fly south of the direct route so as to miss both the stub and Chilbolton, and pick up the A34 south of the service station. By aiming-off in this fashion I would not have to wonder which way to turn to find the service station on reaching the A34.

VFR FLIGHT LOG

Airplan Flight Equipment
1a Ringway Trading Est. Manchester M22 5LH
Tel: 0161 499 0023 Fax: 0161 499 0298
www.afeonline.com

DATE **19/05 page 1**

PILOT **SELF**	A/C **G-BB2H**	ALTERNATE **WHITE WALTHAM EGLM**	
FROM **EXETER** **EGTE**		DISTANCE **42**	FLIGHT TIME **20**
TO **STAPLEFORD** **EGSG**		SUNSET **1939**	VAR. **4-5°W**

DISTANCE **158**	FLIGHT TIME	**1:25**	2000' w/v **060/15**		TEMP. **+07**
F FUEL	FUEL CONSUMPTION	**40L**	5000' w/v **065/20**		**+01**
R RADIO	TOTAL REQUIRED	**70**	DEPARTURE INFO.		
E ENGINE	FUEL ON BOARD	**190**			
D DIRECTION	RESERVE	**120**			
A ALTIMETER	TOTAL ENDURANCE	**4:45**			

BRAKES OFF | TAKE OFF | LANDING | BRAKES ON

FROM/TO	MSA	PL/ALT	TAS	TR(T)	W/V	HDG(T)	HDG(M)	G/S	DIST	TIME	ETA	ATA
Exeter ——— Axminster	2600	2000	125	080	060/15	077	082	111	16	9		
Axminster S.AgveSALISBURY ①	2200	2000	125	073	060/15	071	075	110	48	27		
S.AgveSALISBURY Sutton Scotney ②	1700	2000	125	066	060/15	066	070	110	18	10		
Sutton Scotney ——— Newbury ③	2300	2000	125	360	060/15	006	010	116	14	7		
——— Continued on page 2					/							
———					/							

DISTRESS 121.50 | TRANSPONDER | DISTRESS 7700 | COM FAIL 7600 | CONSPICUITY 7000

STATION	SVC	FREQ.	CLEARANCE/OBSERVATIONS
Exeter	TWR	119.8	① SAM 113.35 R290 18 d
	Appr	128.15	② SAM 113.35 R005 12d
Yeovilton	Radar	127.35	③ CPT 114.35 R229 6.8d
C.Abbas	Radio	122.70	
Boscombe	Radar	126.70	
Solent	Appr	120.225	
Farnborough	Radar	125.25	

NAUTICAL MILES 1:500,000

PLOG for the route (page 1)

VFR FLIGHT LOG

Airplan Flight Equipment
1a Ringway Trading Est. Manchester M22 5LH
Tel: 0161 499 0023 Fax: 0161 499 0298
www.afeonline.com

DATE 19/05 page 2					
PILOT **SELF**	A/C **G-BB2H**		ALTERNATE **WHITE WALTHAM EGLM**		
FROM **EXETER** **EGTE**			DISTANCE **42**	FLIGHT TIME **20**	
TO **STAPLEFORD** **EGSG**			SUNSET **1939**	VAR. **4–5°W**	
DISTANCE **158**	FLIGHT TIME	**1:25**	2000' w/v **060/15**		TEMP. **+07**

F FUEL	FUEL CONSUMPTION	**40L**	5000' w/v **065/20**	**+01**
R RADIO	TOTAL REQUIRED	**70**	DEPARTURE INFO.	
E ENGINE	FUEL ON BOARD	**190**		
D DIRECTION	RESERVE	**120**		
A ALTIMETER	TOTAL ENDURANCE	**4:45**		

BRAKES OFF	TAKE OFF	LANDING	BRAKES ON

FROM/TO	MSA	PL/ALT	TAS	TR(T)	W/V	HDG(T)	HDG(M)	G/S	DIST	TIME	ETA	ATA
Newbury **Henley-on-Thames** ④	2200	2000	125	069	060/15	068	072	110	19	10		
Henley-on-Thames **BNN 113.75**	2200	2000	125	047	060/15	048	052	110	17	9		
BNN 113.75 **Stapleford EGSG**	2000	2000	125	100	060/15	095	099	114	26	14		
————												
————												
————												

DISTRESS 121.50   TRANSPONDER   DISTRESS 7700   COM FAIL 7600   CONSPICUITY 7000

STATION	SVC	FREQ.	CLEARANCE/OBSERVATIONS
Farnborough	Radar	125.25	④ CPT 114.35 R089 12d
Benson	Radar	120.9	
Wycombe	Appr	126.55	
Luton	Radar	129.55	
Stansted	ATIS	127.17	
Essex	Radar	120.625	
Stapleford	Info	122.80	
W.Waltham	Radio	122.60	

PLOG for the route (page 2)

I chose Newbury as my next waypoint – easy to find by just following the A34 northwards. I reckoned to turn north-east here and strike out across the northern edge of Reading to find Henley just south of the distinctive U-bend in the Thames. The next waypoint would be the M40 between High Wycombe and Beaconsfield. This is another pinch-point, with the London TMA on your right and Wycombe Air Park ATZ on your left.

I am not all that familiar with east Buckinghamshire and Hertfordshire from the air, and visual navigation is complicated by the mass of detail with no clearly distinguishable line features. The many features visible can easily be confused by a stranger. So I elected to choose Bovingdon and Lambourne VOR/DMEs for my last two waypoints. My track would take me clear of the Luton control area and Elstree ATZ: it was sufficiently far north of the London conurbation for me to be able to avoid settlements if flying low-level by threading my way between them.

The night before

I obtained NOTAMs and had a preliminary look at the weather. There was nothing to affect apart from a gliding competition at Lasham. Even without a competition, Lasham is usually busy and gliders are practically invisible head-on or tail-on – so it is an airfield I always try to avoid in any case.

I needed to be at Stapleford at about 1100 local. The flight would take a maximum of an hour and a half. I would want to be at Exeter Airport half an hour before take-off, and it would take another half an hour to get there from home. So I needed to set off at 0830 local. If my ETA at Stapleford had been critical I would have allowed an extra half-hour and set off at 0800. Allowing time for getting the met and final flight planning, and something for getting up and eating breakfast, I set the alarm for 0730.

So I would be leaving home at 0830 to be 235 statute miles away by 1100. The alternative of driving there, even with motorway all the way, would take me an hour more (always providing that the M25 was clear) and would be far more tiring than flying. I would not have viewed a drive home again on the same day with any enthusiasm at all. My case rests: for long journeys the aeroplane is a seriously useful form of personal transport.

On the Day

The forecast was for a light north-easterly wind and good visibility. The forecast cloudbase varied from 2000ft in the west to scattered at 1000ft and broken at 1500ft in the east. This was within my personal minima. The outlook was for some improvement, so there should not be a problem in getting back in the afternoon. No TAF was available for Stapleford early in the morning but the TAF for Stansted nearby was: TAF EGSS 130600Z 130716 05010 9999 SCT008 BKN014 TEMPO 0912 04015 9999 -SHRA SCT005 BKN010

This decodes as: *Nine-hour TAF issued at 0600 on the 13th, valid from 0700 until 1600 for Stansted. Wind 050° at 10kts. Over 10 kilometres visibility. Scattered cloud, base 800ft, broken cloud, base 1400ft. Temporarily at any time between 0900 and 1200, wind 040° at 15kts. Over 10 kilometres visibility. Slight rain showers. Scattered cloud, base 500ft, broken cloud, base 1000ft.*

Stapleford is about 150ft lower than Stansted, so the cloudbase should be no worse at Stapleford than at Stansted and might be slightly better. The general conditions looked acceptable but the TEMPO could present a problem. I was not familiar with Stapleford and it is mostly grass, so would probably be difficult to identify from the air. However, with the aid of the Lambourne VOR at only 450m from the threshold of runway 04 at Stapleford, I thought it should not prove too difficult to find. TEMPO conditions are forecast not to exceed half an hour, so I could if necessary stand off waiting for an improvement. I would fill the tanks full, which would give me 4·5h endurance at maximum cruise. This would be plenty to stand-off for half an hour, or to divert to somewhere to await better weather. With IFR capability this could be Stansted but for VFR there are several airfields around; the further west I retreated, the better weather conditions were likely to be. If necessary I could divert all the way back to Exeter without refuelling.

So the decision was Go!

I faxed my booking out details to Exeter, fed the winds into the whizzy wheel and completed my navigation plot.

The Flight

Weather conditions permitted the direct route along the railway line to Axminster and I followed this without incident, except that on reaching Axminster – which is a VRP (Visual Reference Point) and getting near the extreme range for low-level radio contact with Exeter – I called them and reported that I was 1500ft passing *Axbridge,* a town some 30nm to the north of Axminster.

"I think you mean Axminster", said the approach controller. I agreed with him.

I was now embarked on a long leg across Dorset to Salisbury, most simply achieved by following the railway line. Naturally you check your heading to see that you are following the right railway line in the right direction. It is not true, incidentally, that IFR stands for "I Follow Railways". You tick off the major towns and take care to skirt around settlements and to avoid the ATZs of any airfields. With the ADF I would be able to get confirmation of progress as I passed Yeovil and Compton Abbas.

A prospect of Salisbury from DME 18 on the 290° Radial from SAM

When following line features, make sure you have the right one. It is all too easy to fly down the wrong railway line, which by Sod's Law will lead directly into Class A airspace and embarrassment all round. So having found your railway, do not slip your mind into neutral. Instead, check that the heading is what you would expect if you were flying the right railway and check off the features that you encounter along it against your map.

With an actual cloudbase of 2500ft in the west and good visibility, the first half of the flight was easy. Knowing the terrain between Exeter and Bournemouth fairly well, I actually abandoned the railway line and routed direct to just south of Salisbury at 2000ft. Exeter gave me a radar information service to start with but after passing Axminster (not Axbridge) I had to make do with listening out to Yeovil – apparently closed, it being a weekend – and getting a flight information service as I passed Compton Abbas. From

2000ft I scarcely needed confirmation as I approached it that the county town to the north with the splendid spire and the distinctive railway pattern was indeed Salisbury. At a lower height and/or with poorer visibility, I might well have been glad of the VOR/DME's confirmation that I was where I thought I was. Assuming, that is, that the radial from SAM had showed about 290° and the distance about 18nm.

From here on the cloudbase began to lower and I had to descend in stages with it. From south of Salisbury I picked up the tributary with the railway line alongside it and followed them as far as the junction with the River Test. Calling Solent Control as soon as I was within radio range, which was south of Salisbury, I explained my intended route and asked for a radar information service. The 'intention' part of my call went as follows:

> *"I am following the railway line eastwards from Salisbury to 3 miles north-west of Romsey at 1200ft on 1004. I shall then route to Sutton Scotney service area. Squawking 7000."*

The VOR/DME co-ordinates for south abeam Salisbury

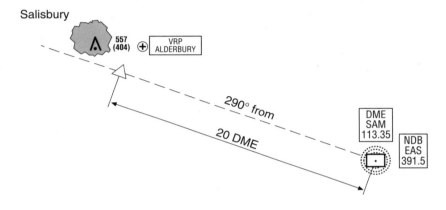

The route from Alderbury to Sutton Scotney

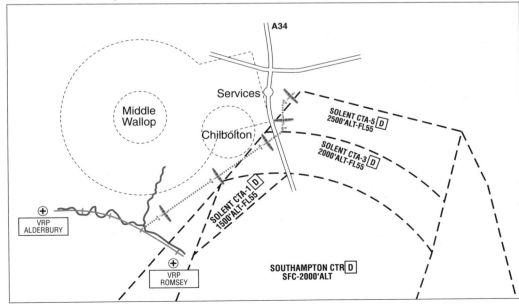

Sutton Scotney Service Area

Initially I was too far away from Southampton and too low for a radar information service, but they now knew who I was and where I was intending to go. As I got closer to their control area, they were able to give me the desired RIS. Note that as I did not intend to enter their area, there was no obligation to call them: some pilots who are afraid of radios and controllers would opt for slipping silently by. If they have a radio, they are foolish to do so. The route to Sutton Scotney is difficult with no obvious visual references, and it would be all too easy to stray inadvertently into the Solent CTA or the Boscombe MATZ. If you are already in touch with Solent and you have fully informed them about your intentions, they will put you right before you have a chance to go seriously wrong. But if you are one of those who prefers to play grandmother's footsteps, you will cause much confusion, aggravation or even worse when – sooner or later – you get it a bit wrong and there is no-one to sort you out in time. Of course, there are times and places when area controllers are too busy to look out for aircraft skirting around them. I would never call Gatwick, for example, except in emergency. In other cases it is advisable to listen out first to make sure that ATC is not too busy to attend to those outside the control area.

Note also that I gave the controller neither heading nor speed in my call, although strictly speaking these should form part of every initial position report. If you are following a line feature, tell the controller that this is what you are doing and he will then know what to expect. If you give your heading at the time of your call, you will only cause surprise later when your heading changes as you follow the feature. In business you should never surprise your bank manager; in the air the same holds good for the controller. So forget blind observance of the rules and instead make sure that you have explained adequately all the relevant facts about your position and intentions. Unless there is something unusual about your speed in relation to your aircraft type, this seems to me to be a redundant piece of information for low-level VFR flying. However, I used regularly to fly a very slippery motor glider, and in that case I would always report "105kts" because the controller would expect such a machine to be cruising at about half that figure.

The important point about your call to the controller – in this and every case – is to be sure to explain just what is going on now and what your real intentions are. Suppose that you are approaching an airfield from the north and you estimate that you have five minutes to run, but you are really not too sure exactly where you are just now. Reject the temptation to sound all professional with phraseology such as "We're ten miles north of you at this time and estimate your field at one seven." That is a thoroughly *unprofessional* call to make in the circumstances. It may well lead to a further exchange which will reveal to all that you are not only a lost pilot, but, much worse, a lost and pretentious pilot. Much better to make a call such as "I estimate that I am ten miles north of you but have not fixed my position yet."

Now that the controller knows the real state of affairs, he is not going to be all that surprised if subsequently you call and say that you have at last fixed your position four miles to the south-west. Yes, it happens. In the meantime the controller may well be able to offer some practical help – perhaps with a radar fix, a QDM, or a helpful query such as "Can you see two tall factory chimneys?". He might even, as a Welsh controller once did, offer to step outside the tower to see if he could hear me.

Beyond Sutton Scotney and with Boscombe, Farnborough and Benson all closed for the weekend, I changed first to Popham and later to White Waltham. Both were fairly busy and I listened-out only so as to get some idea of local traffic. I reminded myself that this could not give the full picture and that a good and conscientious lookout was my best protection. In between these two channels I listened to Volmet South to get Stansted's latest weather. It was important to do this now because I already knew that there was worse weather ahead. If the Stansted actual was unfavourable, it would make much more sense to divert to White Waltham now rather than blunder on into some murk, turn round and blunder out again. On the ground at White Waltham I could monitor the weather further east, press on if it improved as forecast or go home if it did not. Meanwhile White Waltham would be a comfortable and friendly place to have lunch if needs be.

The Stansted actual was scattered at 900ft and broken at 1500ft, so it was slightly better than the general TAF and clearly not experiencing the nastier 'TEMPO' conditions at the time of the report. This seemed to indicate that it was acceptable to continue. However, the weather around Reading was significantly worse than I had been experiencing down west. The main cloudbase was now at 2000ft with some scattered stratus with base 800ft and tops 1200ft. I could not expect to continue below the 800ft scattered base without breaking the 500ft rule in places. Furthermore, at this height my range of vision would make visual navigation impractical over strange territory without usable line features. So if I was to continue at all, it would have to be above the scattered stratus and below the main base. Even scattered clouds beneath you make visual navigation difficult.

Without either prominent and continuous visual features to follow or radio aids as back-up, I would not attempt visual navigation over strange terrain. In this case however, I had Bovingdon and Lambourne VOR/DMEs to supplement my visual sightings; with these aids, I expected to manage well enough in the expected conditions. However, there was one more question to ask myself at this point, and this was whether I had a way out if things should turn nasty. I knew from the Stansted TAF as well as from the general forecast that there was a risk of running into showers with cloud down to the hilltops in places. At the same time the stratus tops could reach all the way up to the main cloudbase, and what would poor pilot do then? True, such conditions were forecast not to exceed more than half an hour at a time. However, half an hour in such conditions would seem more like a lifetime if I was to end up blundering around a few hundred feet above north London's rooftops in poor visibility.

So for a strictly VFR pilot and/or aircraft, there would be no acceptable way out if the TEMPO conditions proved to be prevalent. That being the case, it would be stupidly risky for the VFR pilot to continue. Of course if they did, avoided the showers and arrived without incident at Stapleford, the world might think that the outcome vindicated the decision. But if you load one bullet into a revolver with six chambers, spin them, fire the revolver at your head and survive, does the world then think that your survival has vindicated your action?

Fortunately for me, the aircraft and I were cleared for IFR and I was in good instrument-flying practice. So that was my way out if things should turn nasty. If the cloud tops beneath me should start to merge with the main cloudbase above me, and if there was no retreat back the way I had come, I could always enter IMC and climb at once to minimum safety height. I could call Luton or Stansted and request an instrument approach to either field. That would be an immensely safer strategy than groping about just above those metropolitan rooftops.

So from Newbury I found my way around the northern boundary of Reading and aimed a bit south of Henley so that I would be sure not to miss the Thames altogether.

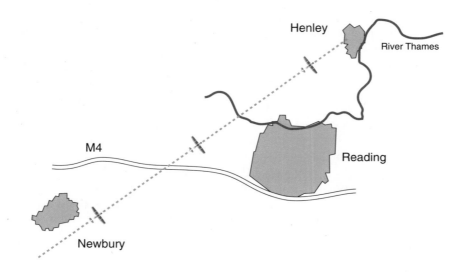

The route from Newbury to Henley

The route past Wycombe Air Park

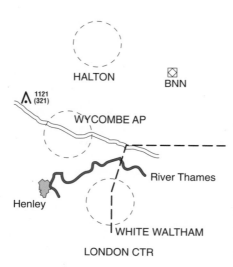

The low-level route beyond Henley takes you through the narrow rat-run between the south-eastern boundary of Wycombe Air Park ATZ and the north-western corner of the London CTR. The gap is only 1·5nm across and you should not attempt it unless you are quite confident of your position and in good visibility. In theory, you might imagine that you could fly 045° TO the BNN VOR and pop through the middle of the gap. But in practice you would be unwise to put such faith in the accuracy of the VOR system. It is not for nothing that the airways, navigated principally by flying from one VOR to the next, are all of ten miles wide. The best accuracy you can expect of the VOR system is within five degrees, and I have often seen two VORs on the same aircraft differ by more than this. So I should not like to rely on a VOR to keep me in the centre of such a tight and crucial gap at ten miles range from the beacon. In the now difficult weather I was unhappy about attempting this gap and the alternative of flying west about the Wycombe ATZ seemed more sensible. The problem here would be the Chilterns to the west of Wycombe. They rise to 837ft and a radio mast rising to 1121ft stands on top. However, with the main cloudbase still at 1700ft it was feasible to overfly this point in VMC on top of the scattered stratus below.

At Henley I had called Luton for a radar information service. "I am routing west of Wycombe and then via Bovingdon", I told them. They gave me a squawk and the radar information service requested. I intended to turn towards the Bovingdon VOR when abeam the radio mast which would come up just after crossing the M40. However, I must have missed both amongst the scattered stratus beneath because Luton called, "Your vector for Stapleford is now 100° and if you go further north you will enter the Halton ATZ." So I thanked them and turned east towards Stapleford, grateful that their monitoring of my progress had kept me out of trouble.

I found that I could raise Lambourne VOR at this range, so I confirmed the ident, checked that the flags were away and set the OBS to 100° with TO showing. This confirmed the radar vector and I continued merrily on my way. I kept the bar central on the CDI by remembering that the bar shows you where the track has got to; so if it is out to the right a bit you need to turn right a bit to recapture it. At the same time I remembered that the VOR's function was to act as an aid to my visual navigation. With a DME readout to assist as well, it was fairly easy to identify the various visual features as they passed beneath.

I passed south of Hemel Hempstead and north of Watford, where I identified the M25. I stayed with Luton Radar until at 7 DME from Lambourne, with much reduced airspeed and a notch of flap, I thanked them and called Stapleford for joining instructions. These were runway 22 left-hand and nothing else in the circuit. Pressing on direct for Lambourne on the 100° TO track gave me a glimpse of the airfield in my eleven o'clock at about 2 DME. Keeping this in sight all the time, I put down the wheels and some more flap and dropped beneath the scattered cloudbase for a low-level circuit and landing.

Post-flight Assessment

Post-flight Assessment

Unless you have reached that dangerous stage where you imagine that you have nothing more to learn – and that is a very dangerous stage indeed – you should always make a practice of examining every flight in the aftermath to see what can be learned and used another time. Consider what went wrong and what turned out differently from what was planned or expected. Also consider what surprised or upset ATC, your fellow crew members or your passengers. Reflect also on what went right, what went entirely according to plan and what seemed to leave all others involved generally contented.

Where something went wrong, decide why this came about, how you might have done it differently and how you will approach the situation next time. Did you choose the wrong route? Was there a fault or oversight in your pre-planning? Did you fail to check something during the flight? Did you find yourself getting behind the aeroplane? Did you become overloaded?

All these sort of occurrences need careful examination with a view to getting to the bottom of the matter. You become a sort of one-person Air Accident Investigation Board, holding an inquiry into yourself and your performance. The Board's determination will probably point as usual to pilot error, but you need to go further than this and ask yourself why it was that you erred. It is very important at such times to realise that while pilot error is a neat solution to queries about anything which goes wrong in the air, your personal inquiry needs to investigate the circumstances which led to the error.

> *Overload?*
> Arrange matters in future so that you don't have so much to do at once.
>
> *Misheard instructions?*
> Did you write down and read back? Are your radio and headset really up to the mark?
>
> *Forgot to check something?*
> Review your checking procedures and revise if necessary.
>
> *Out of practice?*
> Get some in, perhaps with a good instructor.

And so on: the list is endless. But do remember that (contrary to what the official publications may lead you to imagine) pilots, controllers, engineers and everybody else associated with aviation are making mistakes all day and every day. So there is no need to feel ashamed if your own performance was less than perfect. Try to learn each time from your mistakes and you will certainly continue to improve – but if you are human you will never, ever become a perfect pilot .

As far as my flight from Exeter to Stapleford described in the last chapter was concerned, the major subject of interest at the self-debriefing was the failure to identify the waypoint at the radio mast just beyond Wycombe Air Park and change heading. On reflection, I decided that the principal cause was my failure to use timing to monitor distance along track. I had noted my time at the Henley-on-Thames waypoint at 0937. It was about eight miles to the radio mast which, at a ground speed of around 120kts, would take about four minutes. So I could expect to be over the radio mast at around 0941. I should have made myself aware of this – and if I had not identified the mast by 0942, I would know that I had passed it unseen and would have turned towards Bovingdon. Alternatively, I could have set the desired track to BNN of 100° on the OBS of the VOR, tuned it to BNN, identified it and then observed the CDI showing the desired track TO crossing the CDI from left to right. Then I could have turned towards the beacon as the needle came central. The timing alternative is probably simpler and therefore better, but the important point identified by the Board of Enquiry (in this case me) is that I failed to use either. Instead I relied on identifying the mast visually when I knew that this could be tricky because of the intervening scattered cloud, and I put no navigational check in place. With the benefit of hindsight I could see that I had been careless and had exercised poor judgement. The resolve was to be more rigorous in future in using timing as a fundamental aid, and I noted that once again I had been saved from myself by a radar controller.

So, as the man said, you learn something every day.

What went well during your flight calls for your attention just as much. By now you will be accomplishing some tasks as though they are second nature, but there will be others where getting it entirely right is altogether a new experience. As strange as it sounds, you need to review why it is that all is now going well. Perhaps you have consciously adopted some new technique, in which case you now have evidence of its efficacy. Perhaps you are not quite sure why you have found a new felicity with some task; it can be very useful to try to analyse why this should be so. In this way you should be able to discover how to repeat your recent success at will.

Flying is partly about seat-of-the-pants handling together with hand and eye co-ordination, but it is also about being thoughtful and searching all the time for better ways of doing things. It is no accident that better than average pilots usually have better than average intelligence. A lot of the best flying goes on in the head, so take the opportunity to relive all your flights to see what you can learn from each one of them.

"Flying…is also about being thoughtful…"

Going Foreign

Going Foreign

If most light aircraft were made for travel, it must follow for the private pilot based in the UK that travelling abroad is a privilege and a pleasure which is not be missed. Island race that we Britons are, it is inevitable that foreign travel involves crossing water, and here the light aircraft really comes into its own. You have to operate quite a fast aircraft to travel significantly more quickly than you could drive on our motorways. The preparation times involved, the uncertainty over the weather, the restriction of airfield opening times and the lack of personal transport (beyond, perhaps, a folding bicycle) at your destination greatly handicaps flying by light aircraft as a rival to driving by motorway. For my part, I tend to start thinking about flying rather than driving if the destination exceeds 100 miles off-motorway and 200 miles on-motorway. I have to admit, however, that these figures are artificially low because of a love of flying for its own sake. For true time and cost-efficiency you probably have to double those figures.

But once you start to look at crossing water, the light aeroplane begins to make a lot of sense. So whether you are thinking of crossing the Channel, the Irish Sea or merely visiting one of our offshore islands, you will find that a flight by light aircraft is usually quicker, more convenient, less tiring and often cheaper compared with the alternatives. In the recent past I have visited the Channel Islands, the Isle of Mull, the Isles of Scilly, Lundy Isle, Ireland, France, Belgium, Holland, Germany, the Czech Republic and Spain by air. That is not a noteworthy list by any means, and I know private pilots who have been to most of the eastern European countries, Italy, Greece and northern Africa. My own foreign travels have been enormously enjoyable, as have those of all my acquaintances. The cost has been modest and the convenience impressive.

For example, from the south of England you can fly to La Rochelle, half-way down the Bay of Biscay coast, in less than three hours in most light aircraft. For a part-owner of a modest four-seater the cost per hour wet will work out at perhaps £70. Six hours there and back will come out at £420 and there will be a surprisingly small landing fee, which will be more than offset by the value of the fuel drawback. So at a cost of £105 per head you can fly to La Rochelle and back, taking less than half a day door-to-door. Do you know of an easier or cheaper way of taking French leave? Many of my travels abroad have been in a slower two-seater, but while the journeys take about 30% longer in flying time, you are still way ahead of other forms of transport.

Apart from the convenience and the modest cost, the flights have been enormous fun: much easier than I imagined at first and very satisfying. For these reasons therefore I recommend going foreign as perhaps the most rewarding goal of any PPL. If you can cope with flying around the UK you should have no serious problems abroad. "Over there" the language of air traffic control is still English, and flying is often noticeably less restricted than it is in the UK.

Because information is more difficult to get hold of, it is as well to start preparations for foreign travel well in advance. Starting a month ahead would be comfortable if you are going somewhere new to you.

The rewards of a successful voyage. A group on a flyout enjoy a much deserved harbourside drink at Honfleur

Maps and Flight Guides

The first step is to borrow or buy aeronautical maps and a flight guide. You will need the current editions – so find out the publication date of updates of whatever you want, wait until that day comes around and then make quite sure that you get the latest edition and not the previous one. For VFR flying you will need half-million maps for your entire route. If you are going to visit more than one country and there is a choice of map publishers, you may like to standardise where possible on one. Jeppesen or the USAF series are the likely possibilities, and sticking with either should prevent confusion from differing presentations. This is particularly so where you find one map-maker showing heights in feet and another in metres, for example. Similar considerations apply to flight guides, although the only Europe-wide VFR flight-guide series currently available is the Bottlang – expensive, but very thorough.

Having acquired your maps and flight guides, the time has come to spend lots of absorbing time getting to know them. By now you are no doubt well acquainted with the British half-million maps and you probably use one of the popular British flight guides as well. The equivalents used abroad contain at least as much information, but it is set out in a different manner. It is a great mistake to set off to somewhere strange using maps and guides with which you are not at all familiar. Doing so will greatly add to your workload, and quite unnecessarily because you can so easily spend a useful few evenings poring over your foreign maps and guides so that their systems of presentation become entirely familiar to you.

While maps and flight guides will tell you all you need to know while airborne, do not lose sight of the point that your flying is not likely to be an end in itself. It certainly will not be so for your passengers. Flying is a convenient way to get from A to B – but if B turns out to be dull, unfriendly and/or unreasonably expensive, the trip will not be a success. So you need to find out which destinations are likely to suit you and your passengers. Magazines such as Today's *Pilot*, *Flyer* and club newsletters frequently publish descriptions by contributors of touring flights made around Europe. These are useful sources of information about good and bad places to visit. Asking around amongst more experienced touring pilots is always worthwhile, and raising queries on appropriate newsgroups on the Internet will often bring in plenty of useful information. You should cast the net a good deal wider than flying magazines, however. The point of the exercise is to go somewhere interesting and attractive as a holiday destination, not just somewhere where there is a convenient airfield. So find destinations that have something to offer in their own right and then set about seeing how best to get there by air. Local knowledge is often enormously helpful and the Internet is probably the best source.

If all the occupants of the aircraft are pilots, a more vagabond style of travel may suit. The itinerary can be constructed on the hoof as the weather, whim and other circumstances may direct.

Range

When you have trawled in enough particulars about destinations and decided where you want to go, the time comes to work out your route. A crucial factor here will be the range of your aircraft, and in many cases this will involve decisions about trading fuel capacity for people and/or baggage-carrying capacity. The issue to be addressed is the useful load of your aircraft and just what you intend to load it with. If you are not familiar with such calculations, consult the POH/FM and also find out the actual basic weight of your particular aircraft, for which there should be a Weight Schedule.

Estimate the weight of the occupants and the baggage and you will end up with a calculation something like this:

Max All-Up Weight		2400lb
LESS		
Basic Wt of AC	1587lb	
Jim (fully dressed)	180lb	
Joanna (ditto – she's a big girl!)	155lb	
Me (honestly!)	175lb	
The dinghy	25lb	
Spare oil, pickets, flight bag, etc. in the baggage locker	8lb	
Personal baggage:		
3 x 20lb	60lb	
Total wt excl fuel		2190lb
Balance available for fuel		210lb

Assuming that you don't use the pound as your usual unit of fuel, you now need to find out how much 210lb of AVGAS is in litres or whatever you measure your fuel in. Personally I prefer to work in litres because that is how you buy it at the pumps, and it avoids the dangerous confusion which always lurks as regards US gallons and Imperial gallons.

Time to get out the whizzy wheel. First of all you convert 210lb to its equivalent in kilograms. It comes to 91kg. Now if AVGAS had the same density as water, a mass of 91kg would equal 91ltr in volume. Actually AVGAS has a specific gravity of 0·72. So divide this into 91, or place 91 on the inner scale against 72 on the outer (where you will find 'Sp G' marked) and read off against the 10 on the outer scale at the top of the wheel. We end up with an equivalent volume of 126ltr.

So 126ltr of fuel (or 28imp gal, or 33US gal) is going to be the most you can load up, even if your tanks will actually hold more. Similarly, if the maximum fuel allowed by this calculation exceeds your tank capacity, you can afford to increase the other loadings.

Remember to carry out a balance calculation for this loading, both fully loaded and also with the tanks empty and the heaviest passenger(s) in the back seat. If both calculations are within limits, all likely C of G variations should have been covered.

This passenger knows that keeping her flight bag on her lap will not reduce the total weight. Some others are not so smart

You may be taking a passenger like one with whom I regularly have the pleasure of flying – who thinks that something heavy carried as hand luggage on her lap does not affect the total weight, although it would do so if carried in her main luggage. Make due allowances for such folk. The same passenger has a regrettable tendency to return home with rather more baggage than she set out with. You may also have to make allowance for this…

Establish how much your maximum fuel load is going to be and then address the question of range with this fuel load. For VFR flying a reserve of 30 minutes is often taken as appropriate, but when flying to a strange destination I would personally regard 45min as desirable. In addition, do not forget to add a factor of 10% to your consumption against worse than forecast headwinds. Pick an alternate along the route, so that you can make an earlier fuel stop if you find that consumption is working out higher than planned. Study the map and flight guide as regards your alternate to precisely the same extent as you will no doubt study them in relation to your proposed destinations.

I'm sure you know how to do fuel-consumption calculations, but here is a typical example just in case the technique has slipped your mind:

Proposed Flight
from Southampton to Rennes, via Cherboug:

Distance		185nm
Ground Speed: TAS +/- forecast headwind		100kts
Consumption	Climb power	30ltr/hr
	75% Cruise	23ltr/hr
	65% Cruise	19ltr/hr
Taxi out and take-off. Say		10ltr
Climb to 5000ft	10min @ 30ltr/hr	5ltr
Cruise @ 75%	104min (173nm @ 100kts)	40ltr
Reserve	45min @ 19ltr/hr	14ltr
	Sub-total	69ltr
Factor for unforecast headwind	10%	7ltr
Total Required		76ltr

If that total is not within the tanks or your weight limitations, you must either shorten the leg by stopping *en route* or lighten the load so as to take on more fuel.

If you tour is going to involve several legs, it makes sense to work out what your maximum range is with the proposed load of people and baggage on board. Make the allowances described above, assume nil wind and that you will fill up with the lesser of a) full tanks or b) the maximum fuel load available within your weight limitations. If this comes to say 320nm, you know this is the maximum sector length you can consider in still air.

Long-distance touring calls for decisions as to how much flying you and your passengers want to do in a day. Passengers who are not pilots are usually unhappy flying for more than three or four hours a day because long flights tend to get boring and uncomfortable for them. If you get the flying out of the way by lunch-time, even though this entails an early start, that will leave the rest of the day at the next destination for disporting yourselves on *terra firma*. Thus may you avoid the charge of submitting your non-piloting passengers to a holiday of all flying and no fun. In hotter climes it may also get you down on the ground before a regular build-up of thunderstorms in the afternoon.

Apart from any possible lack of enthusiasm for flying on the part of some passengers, you should also plan to allow for the fact that VFR flying is distinctly weather-dependent – especially when flying over strange territory. If it needs six or eight hours of flying to get home again and one of you has to be back by a given date without fail, give yourself two or three days for the journey. If the weather seems set fair on the penultimate day, you can always get 'nearly' home and spend the last night still abroad but close to home. If the weather turns doubtful towards the end of your holiday, you may find yourself hanging around the met office waiting for an improvement to within your personal minima. The nearer you are to home at such a juncture, the more likely you are to be able to make it. Failing that, it's always worth planning so that someone who absolutely *has* to get back on time can use public transport as a last resort.

The Weather

You are of course used to getting the weather before each flight in the UK. For a flight abroad you may be able to use your usual source if your destination is close to Britain. Once you are abroad and looking for further weather information, you will have to fit in with whatever system is on offer for local private pilots. The good news is that for most western European countries this is usually at least as good as what is on offer in the UK, and in many it is both better and cheaper.

Your primary source of information about how to get the weather is your flight guide, and a careful reading of the Meteorology section is important – as is a close perusal of the General, Communications, Regulations and Aerodromes sections. Always remember that while acquiring an up-to-date flight guide is an essential, you must also go through it carefully during the days or weeks before your flight so as to brief yourself properly in advance. Just chucking the new guide into your flight bag and hoping to pick up the necessary information as you go along is not a good idea. The arrangements for obtaining weather information vary a good deal between one country and another. The large airports usually have good briefing facilities, often with English-speaking staff. A useful source of *en route* weather information is Volmet, which will always offer actuals in English for the leading airfields in any country. Make sure that you have the appropriate frequencies with you. The latest edition of the communications booklet published by Aerad is a useful source; look under the listings for the international airports and you will find the weather frequency.

Getting the weather at a small airfield or (even worse) from your hotel, presents more of a challenge if you do not have access to the internet. In France there is the Minitel service, which will tell you all you need if only you can fathom out how to use it. My usual solution is to find a helpful French person, show him or her the flight guide instructions and the Minitel machine and ask for help. Alternatively in France you can get a weather fax, but you will need a personal access code. You have to write off for this with a copy of your licence to SCEM/OSAS/TE, 42 avenue Gustave Coriolis, F-31057 TOULOUSE Cédex. So here is just one example of the value of doing your homework before you go. Without your previously obtained personal access code, the fax system will be denied to you.

In Belgium you phone the nearest Met office. In Ireland you can call Shannon where, like as not, you will find a friendly met officer apparently happy to talk to you all day if you wish.

If you can speak the local language and have an up-to-date flight guide, you should encounter no problems. Plan B, if you do not speak the language, is to find a met officer or, failing that, a pilot who speaks English or some other language common between the two of you. Plan C is to do the best you can by making your destination and time of proposed flight known to the met officer or a helpful local pilot. You **must** then get sight of a weather map, METARs and TAFs at least. These may have seemed to be in a foreign language to you once upon a time, but you will now be relieved to find that they are much the same the whole world over. If you can interpret them at home, you can interpret them abroad with equal ease. So don't leave home without being able to understand them. Remember that a TAF and an actual for your destination are insufficient on their own if the destination is more than about fifty miles away. You will be wanting some *en route* information as well.

Rules of the Air

The rules of the air are basically the same abroad as they are at home, but with local variations. The mechanism for this is that there are International Civil Aviation Organisation (ICAO) rules to which all countries subscribe, but individual countries may publish their own divergences from these rules. It is important to appreciate that Britain does not itself follow the ICAO rules entirely. So you will find, for example, that when you get to Holland they do not follow the Quadrantal Height Rule. Instead they have adopted something called the Semi-Circular Height Rule (fly 000° to 179° tracks at odd thousands of feet and 180° to 359° at even thousands). But you would be quite wrong to consider our Dutch friends tiresomely eccentric in this matter. It is in fact the Brits who are out of line, and the Semi-Circular Height Rule is called for by ICAO rules. Indeed, it generally applies throughout continental Europe and the Irish Republic.

Popular areas for confusion between one country's rules and another are:

1   Definition of VMC, especially as regards the permissibility of "VMC on top".

2   The British IMC Rating: this is not recognised outside the UK, which means that even if you have an IMC Rating you will have to maintain VMC at all times outside the UK boundaries.

3   Flying airways: this is permitted VFR in many countries. Where it is, that is how they would prefer you to fly routes. Of those that do, some require you to keep to the specified airway levels (the Semi-Circular Height Rule modified in the case of a few airways as indicated on an airways chart by 'E>'. This requires you to fly the marked section of an airway contrariwise to the usual rule. So tracks between 000° and 179° are to be flown at even thousands of feet and 180° to 359° at odd thousands). Other countries will require VFR users of the airway to fly at 500ft above the usual airway level. See what the flight guide says for your destination country.

4   VFR at night: the rules vary substantially from one country to another.

5   VFR approaches to airfields: these often involve routes in and out via various points similar to our Visual Reference Points, and you will need a flight guide to cope with this. The points are often defined by a 'November, Sierra, Echo, Whisky' system – that is to say one based on north, south, east and west. When the approach controller clears you to "Join via Sierra", you will know that this will be via some landmark to the south of the airfield. However, without a good flight guide you will not know what it is because these points are not usually marked on half-million topo charts.

6   Circuit joining procedure: this varies from country to country. Your flight guide should explain what is usual in a particular country, and it would be unwise to assume that it will be just the same as at home.

The official source of information about the rules governing flight in any country will be the Aeronautical Information Publication (AIP) for that country. The British AIP is the 'Air Pilot', as found at most flying schools and airfield flight-briefing rooms and also available on the NATS website on www.ais.org.uk. You can inspect those for foreign parts at briefing rooms and the like at foreign airfields. Foreign versions are just as wordy and disorganised as our own, and are often in a foreign language to boot. If you want to inspect one before you go, the Foreign Records Section of the Aeronautical Information Service at Heathrow Airport may be able to help but this may be on a self-briefing basis only. Alternately, some are available via the internet. For all but the most punctilious pilot, however, life is too short to get involved in all this for a VFR flight to a nearby country. There is usually enough information in the flight guide for that country to get you by. Furthermore, air traffic controllers and airfield operators are usually friendly, forgiving and helpful to visiting foreign pilots, and are not totally surprised if visitors demonstrate less familiarity with the local rules than an indigenous aviator.

The UK AIP

Radio

English, thankfully, is the common language of the air and we enjoy a tremendous advantage over other European pilots in this respect. How would you fancy learning to navigate and communicate in a foreign tongue? However, the VFR pilot may find that calls in English go unheeded in parts of France, Italy Spain and some other countries. Whilst *en route* and in uncontrolled airspace this usually presents no great problem. You can proceed on your way transmitting blind in English and remembering your responsibility for your own separation from other aircraft. If your calls in English are still ignored on entering controlled airspace, including the ATZ of your destination field, you might try communication in the vernacular. Alternatively you might proceed as though non-radio but continuing to make blind calls in English. In France radio calls in French are mandatory on some of the smaller airfields. A good guide to calls in French is available at www.webvivant.com/aero-andaines. In Belgium, because of antipathy between French and Flemish speakers, it is best to stick to English. In North Western Europe every controller seems to have some English.

Customs and Immigration

If your flight is from one European Union (EU) member country to another, the rules are fairly simple. To depart the UK for another EU member state, you need not inform Customs and Immigration of your intentions. You are not restricted, so far as the British rules are concerned, to a particular point of departure. On return to the UK from an EU member state, you are not restricted as to where you may land. However, you must give advance warning of your flight and you must provide flight-plan details and details of all on board. These details will extend to names, addresses and nationalities.

Even within the EU the Customs and Immigration regulations vary. The general rule regarding international movements requires an arriving or departing crew to clear customs immediately on arrival and before departure. Many EU states are subscribers to the 'Schengen Agreement' wherein, in theory at least, EU citizens may pass from one state to another without any formalities. You should be aware, however, that Britain is not a subscribing state and that some states that are – notably France – do not always seem to honour the agreement. Sometimes they impose penalties even on EU private pilots arriving from other Schengen Agreement states who ignore the usual customs arrangements.

You should first consult the flight guide for your destination country and see what the local requirements are. You may also consult the destination airfield operator, the local flying club and/or a handling agent at the airfield. Unless you have good reason to believe that the rules for non-EU movements will be relaxed in the case of your movement, your best bet is to comply with the general requirements in any case. To do this you will need to find out from the flight guide what the customs facilities are at your proposed destination airfield. Many of the larger ones will have customs presence throughout the operating hours of the airfield; some will have a presence during limited hours and at other times on being given notice. Some airfields will have a customs presence only on notice, and some will have no customs facilities at all. It follows, therefore, that customs facilities on airfields are an important factor in planning your route.

If notice is required, it is important to keep a record of this having been given. A copy of a fax or a letter is ideal, but a note of the exact time of a phone call and to whom it was made is better than nothing.

Many of the larger airfields have handling agents who for a fee will take you under their wing, smooth your passage, see to customs, fuelling, fight planning, surface transport, accommodation and so on. My experience of handling agents varies. On the one hand I have experienced an invaluable service at Biarritz which cost virtually nothing. On the other hand I have used a service on a British airfield which amounted in practice to little more than arranging a taxi into the city at significantly more than the prevailing local cost. And that was for a handling fee of £25.

Running into a problem with customs or immigration officers could spoil your trip entirely and it is therefore worthwhile taking steps to avoid trouble. Unless you are quite sure that there is no need for it, you would do best to arrive at and depart from a customs airfield and to give prior written notice of your movements. Having cleared into a foreign country, be sure to keep the receipt for the landing fee at the airfield of entry. This can then be used to convince customs officers and police at other internal airfields you may visit subsequently that you have already cleared in.

Flight Plan

To cross a national boundary or to cross a stretch of water, you need to file a flight plan. Like so many other things in flying, filling in a flight-plan form seems immensely complicated at first but turns out to be no big deal after the first one or two. However, being something which most VFR pilots do only infrequently, the detailed requirements are soon forgotten and have to be re-acquired on each filing. For that reason I keep a copy of a CAA poster entitled "ICAO Model Flight Plan" and some spare flight-plan forms. An Aeronautical Information Circular entitled "Instructions for Completion of the Flight Plan Form CA48/RAF 2919" will serve equally well. Follow the instructions therein and you will produce a perfect flight plan form every time. If there is a need to clear customs at your destination, it will do no harm to include in Item 18 of the form – Other Information – "REQ CUSTOMS". Opinions differ as to whether this amounts to formal notice to customs, but it can do no harm.

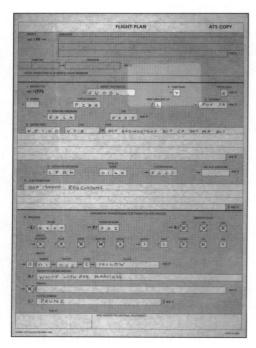

A completed flight plan

It can be a good idea to file your flight plan a day or two in advance, so as to save time and trouble on the day of the flight. You should show the date of the proposed flight in Item 18 – Other Information – as something like: "DOF 060818" (ie. yymmdd). Your estimated Off Block time in Item 13 may be a bit of a guess in advance, but you have half an hour's latitude either way. The total estimated elapsed time on route at item 16 is only an estimate for flight-overdue purposes and does not have to be accurate to the minute. If you have to divert, you must never forget to inform your flight-planned destination airfield of this. Otherwise overdue procedures will be implemented at vast cost. The best way to do the necessary is to request (over the radio) the air traffic controller at your actual landing airfield to inform ATC at your flight-planned destination field of your diversion. Trying to telephone the destination airfield in a foreign country after you have landed may prove much more difficult, and time is of the very essence in this matter.

Other Details

Apart from establishing the availability of customs, if needed, at your destinations, you should also consider fuel if a destination is a proposed fuel stop. In many foreign countries, especially at weekends, fuel becomes unavailable for long periods at lunch time – sometimes for as long as two or three hours. This can turn a "…quick fuel stop" into much pointless hanging around which might have been avoided by a more careful reading of the flight guide in the preparation stage. Check also what sort of payment is required by the fuellers. Some do not accept credit cards, and cash can be a problem if you have just arrived in a country unprepared for this.

Experience has taught me that asking to refuel while taxying in can often save much delay and frustration later. While you are still taxying you have the attention of the tower or ground controller, who will most probably be able to understand your English. Refuelling can thus be simply arranged. But once you have parked, you may find yourself spending a long and frustrating time wandering around the airfield trying to organise refuelling. So resist the temptation to get away to the hotel and its swimming pool as soon as possible and see to the aircraft's needs first.

If you are going to want food, check the flight guide in advance. If you are going to want accommodation, it is usually best to book in advance. Accommodation arranged on spec is seldom up to much in my experience.

Documents

You will need to carry on board a dossier containing:

> Certificate of Registration
>
> Certificate of Airworthiness or Permit to Fly
>
> Aircraft's Flight Manual, with loading schedule for your aircraft
>
> Aircraft's Radio Licence
>
> Certificate of Insurance
>
> General Aviation Safety Sense Leaflet No 11. This tells you what to do when a military aircraft appears in front of you and rocks its wings. Carriage of the leaflet on international flights is mandatory.
>
> Customs General Declaration, if required.
>
> Aircraft Journey Log
>
> Receipt for landing fee at airfield of entry

That is quite a lot of paperwork, but you *must* have it all and you *must* check it to see that it is complete and up to date. In particular, make sure that the insurance covers you for the country being visited and that the liability cover meets that country's requirement, if any. You may fly extensively and never get asked for any papers, but one day you will meet a bureaucrat with a zeal for this sort of thing. If your paperwork is not in good shape, it could easily spoil your whole trip.

In addition, all pilots will need their personal licences and, where appropriate, everybody will need their passports. Taking your driving licences along will avoid problems when it comes to car hire. If you take your AOPA membership or aircrew cards, you may obtain discounts on accommodation and/or car hire.

Fuel Drawback

In case you did not know, I have to tell you that you pay a substantial duty on all the AVGAS you buy in the UK. If, however, you set off to foreign parts with duty-paid fuel in your tanks, you may reclaim the duty on that fuel. Her Majesty's Customs and Excise have managed to turn that simple proposition into a procedure of such complexity that it would be universally ignored were it not for the fact that the "fuel

drawback", as it is known in common parlance can be worth fighting for – especially for those with large tanks. All you will need is form HO60, a fair amount of spare time and the mind of a mandarin.

Form HO60 belongs to an earlier, pre-EU era. A modern Euro-form would be thick with acronyms and have several annexes, but HO60, old-fashioned as it is, seeks to obfuscate with circumlocution. As such forms do, it invites you to seek clarity by consulting the "Notes Overleaf". Naturally the notes overleaf leave you even more baffled. The title alone of HO60 must have greatly accelerated the career of some civil servant towards a well-deserved MBE. It goes "Claim for Drawback of Excise Duty on Hydrocarbon Oil Shipped as Stores on Foreign-going Aircraft." A lesser functionary might have fluffed this valuable opportunity and come up with something wholly inadequate, such as "Fuel Drawback Form", but a real master was at work on HO60.

A completed fuel drawback form

You have to file the form before clearance out, and that may present a problem as clearance is no longer required for flights out to other EU states. I have been known to present the form on my return when clearing in, and I have subsequently been paid, but that may well have been a breach of the letter of the regulations.

Apart from some fairly routine information you are going to need to know:

1 Your tank capacity in litres. Well, you ought to know that already in any case.

2 Your normal consumption per flying hour, also in litres. And that as well.

3 Where and when the fuel in your tanks was bought, who was the supplier, what was the invoice number and how much was supplied. If the fuel on board comes to more than the quantity last supplied you will have to show details of the previous supply as well. If the total from multiple supplies exceeds your total tank capacity, the tank capacity is what you must show as: "Total quantity of fuel loaded."

4 If the last fuel supply was at some airfield before the departure airfield, you have to deduct from the total supplied the amount consumed on the flight(s) thereto.

5 You should now be showing the total in your tanks at departure (excluding any fuel previously purchased abroad), and to that you must apply the going rate of duty per litre, which the Customs office can tell you. You thus arrive at your fuel drawback claim.

I hope you understood all that. In case you did not, let me illustrate with an example. Your tanks hold 200ltr, and you consume 40ltr/hr in the cruise. A week ago the aircraft came back from Guernsey with 150ltr on board. Now that was all purchased abroad, so you are not going to be able to claim drawback on any of it. However the aircraft has been flown since and was refuelled to full tanks at an airfield half an hour's flying time away from your departure field. You have the invoice which shows that 105ltr were taken on at that time. Since then the only flight has been to the departure field which will have consumed 20ltr. Although there are 180ltr in your tanks at departure, you can claim drawback on only:

(105-20) or 85ltr

You leave the form with the customs office and in the fullness of time they should send you a well-earned cheque.

Crossing Water

Going foreign usually involves crossing water, and this calls for extra thought and preparation. You will need to take survival gear and everyone on board is going to need to know how to operate it. In summer the waters around the United Kingdom remain fairly cold – and you should appreciate that it is the cold that represents by far the greatest threat to survival. You may already know that a person immersed in these waters will not survive for more than an hour or two before the cold extinguishes life. However, you may not know that after only ten minutes or so in the summer sea a person may begin to lose the function of the hands. From then on that person is not likely to be able to do much in the way of self-preservation, and thereafter things will only get worse with a progressive loss of the use of limbs and mind. In winter seas these times are substantially shorter.

While you need to give some thought to ditching technique and the wearing of lifejackets, it is not the actual ditching, nor drowning which represent the main threat, but the *cold water*. So the first matter to address is getting help as soon as possible. Initially this will be by way of a Mayday call before ditching, ideally with an accurate fix. You could be very glad of having brought along a Satnav at this point. Next, after ditching, is the deployment of an Emergency Locator Transmitter (ELT). This is likely to foreshorten substantially the time it will take for a SAR helicopter to find you, and remember that time is crucial. Consequently I would regard a good ELT as an essential piece of kit.

Most of us would also prefer to carry a dinghy, but do remember that carrying a dinghy is only half of the story. All of you on board need to know *exactly* how to use it, so that you have a good chance of getting into it while you are still able to do so. If you spend too much time getting the dinghy out of the aircraft, inflating it, righting it and then getting everybody into it, you will lose the ability to finish the task. You will also lose a good deal of body heat and energy in the fruitless attempt. So ideally everyone on board should have done at least one dinghy drill. Failing that ideal, I would regard the dinghy as of doubtful value unless at least half of you have done a drill.

Survival suits are well worth consideration. You can sometimes pick up second-hand ones previously used on oil rigs for quite modest prices. An aircraft with all the occupants wearing survival suits and life jackets equipped with spray hoods, a good-quality dinghy available for immediate deployment and two good-quality ELTs would be my ideal equipment level. However, it is an ideal which I cannot pretend ever to have achieved in practice.

What I have achieved, however, is the use of a schedule of *Dinghy Captain's Duties*, and I have Dr Jan Hedegard, a Swedish safety expert, to thank for this concept. A copy of the schedule that I use appears in the Appendix. At some time before we all do the pre-flight survival equipment briefing, I hand the schedule to my appointed Dinghy Captain and ask him or her to read it. It often gets handed around amongst the other passengers and tends to make all of them think seriously about survival. The appointment of a dinghy captain is a sensible measure. As aircraft captain you may have other priorities during and immediately after ditching, and you need someone to give urgent and proper attention to the deployment of the survival equipment. Furthermore, you may become incapacitated yourself – and if no one else has any idea what to do, all will be lost. The *Dinghy Captain's Duties* sheet is one of the few survival precautions with no weight or cost penalty and yet it makes a material contribution to everybody's chances of survival.

Ditch carefully and you should be unhurt. But how will you all cope with the cold water?

Another valuable safety measure with no significant weight or cost penalty is height. The higher you fly across water, the more time you will have in hand. Time to glide down, summon help, provide an accurate fix; see about a restart, get everybody properly organised, look for a fishing boat to land next to; and work out the most appropriate ditching strategy in the current conditions. The more time you spend up there gliding down, the less time you will have to spend in the water until help arrives. What is more, your forthcoming help will have more notice of your plight. Crossings of the English Channel in uncontrolled airspace used to be seriously height-limited, but sensible amendments have been made recently and VFR crossings are possible at reasonable heights. Currently (2004), for instance, you can usually use the VFR-recommended route across the 52nm from the south of the Isle of Wight to Cherbourg up to FL100. Subject only to the requirements of VMC and the quadrantal height rule (or the semicircular rule on the French side) 10,000ft is the height I should prefer. If your aircraft glides down from up there at 600fpm it will take over 16min between engine failure and ditching. Compared with crossing at sea level, that is 16 extra minutes in the warm and dry for you and 16 extra minutes before you ditch for the helicopter to find you. Furthermore, 16 minutes gliding at say 70kts gives you a glide range in still air of 19nm, which might well be enough to get you to dry land. Effectively your glide range from this height reduces the 52nm sea crossing to only 14nm beyond gliding distance from one shore or another. That is an improvement in the chances of survival which I find impossible to ignore.

Height over the sea is one of those commodities like fuel in your tanks and runway in front of you. All other things being equal, you just can't have too much of it.

The Dinghy Captain gives her survival briefing. Make sure everybody knows what to do after ditching before you take off. It will be too late to brief them later

Is that all?

Is that all?

Well of course it's not. It's just as much as I can get into one book! I have not even mentioned aerobatics, formation flying, seaplanes, precision flying, racing, flying old aircraft, home-building or any of the other strange and fascinating activities that some private pilots get up to. I have dealt mainly with what the large majority of private pilots do, which is using aircraft to go places.

Finally, may I ask you whether you agreed with all I have said in this book?

I do hope the answer is "No". If you have not found anything to disagree with, I suspect you have not been thinking about your flying as deeply as perhaps you should. While you were training, you took in everything the instructors told you as gospel; in theory at least they all sang from the same hymn-book. You may well have found, even during your training, that in practice different instructors have different ways of doing things. Naturally each one will give you convincing arguments as to why their particular way is the best…

Beyond your PPL, where there is no approved syllabus, you will find a much greater diversity of ways of doing things. And you must appreciate that it is you and nobody else in all the world who is the captain of your aircraft. There is no stepladder up to your cockpit with some vastly experienced and omniscient instructor to offer you guidance. There is just you, your aircraft, maybe another crew member and maybe the Fat Controller – if you can get him on your side. So it is mostly, if not entirely, up to your judgement as to which are the right choices. What you have read in this book – or in any other book, or in a flying magazine, or have been told by other pilots or have overheard in the flying-club bar – is all no more than food for thought. The actual thinking has to be done by you because the actual decisions are all down to you as captain.

So agree with me, or disagree. That does not really matter. What matters above all else is that you keep thinking about your flying. How you can make it even safer, and even more fun.

Good luck.

"What matters is that you keep thinking…"

The Night Qualification

The Night Qualification

The JAA Night Qualification calls for five hours of night flying training. Of these, at least three hours must be dual and the solo part must include five solo take-offs and five solo full-stop landings. Three hours of long briefing has to be given as part of the training.

Apart from being the holder of a PPL, there are no other pre requirements.

While the qualification is by no means essential to the VFR pilot it can sometimes come in useful, especially if you do much winter flying.

The IMC Rating

The IMC Rating

This a purely British rating, and is unknown and unrecognised anywhere else. It gives the holder the right to fly in IMC in UK airspace of Class D or less, and also:

- To fly Special VFR in controlled airspace within sight of the surface and in visibility down to 3km (as opposed to 10km for the non IMC Rating holder).
- To fly VFR on top.
- To make instrument landings and take-offs in Class D airspace or less, provided that the visibility is at least 1800m and the cloud base is at least 200ft more than the appropriate minimum for a fully instrument rated pilot.

The pre-requirements are 25 hours experience since gaining a PPL, of which 10 were as PIC. Five of the ten must have been on cross-country flights. However, the 25 hours requirement may include the 15 hours dual training for the Rating. The applicant must also hold a Flight Radiotelephony Operator's licence.

The training comprises 15 hours dual, of which up to two may be on a simulator. At least ten of these hours must be flown by sole reference to the instruments. There are twenty hours of ground studies followed by a ground exam. There is also a flight test.

Opinions differ as to the practical benefits of the IMC Rating for the aeroplane pilot. The argument against it is that it requires insufficient training for a pilot to be able to embark upon a competent and professional IFR flight to a strange airfield and to carry out an instrument approach there. Given its rather restricted use as an emergency back up only, it may seem like a lot of work and expense for not much gain. The CAA discourages pre planned IFR flight by IMC Rating holders, suggesting that its use is only as an emergency resource for the VFR pilot who gets caught out and finds themselves in IMC. Nonetheless, there are occasional accident reports of pilots with IMC Ratings setting off on a pre planned IFR flight and getting into trouble. 'Trouble' for an aeroplane pilot in IMC frequently means a fatality although microlight pilots, with their lower speed and weight, are more likely to survive a crash in IMC.

Having spent some time reading General Aviation accident reports, I have, nonetheless, become a strong advocate of the IMC Rating. The accident reports show that 'VFR into IMC' accidents occur every year and very frequently end in fatalities. While from your armchair it is easy to criticise the VFR-only pilot who flies into cloud, the detailed reports reveals that in many cases becoming IMC was never intended. The atmosphere of the UK does not necessarily consist all the time of clear air interspersed with well defined and easily recognised clouds. Sometimes it is more of a hotch potch of patches of more or less clear air and wispy, ill defined clouds. Furthermore, as many hill walkers will testify, you don't necessarily have to fly, or walk, into a cloud to become IMC; sometimes the cloud just forms around you. So it is not all that uncommon for UK pilots to find themselves inadvertently in cloud.

A pilot with an IMC Rating, even if it has lapsed, and an IFR equipped aeroplane, will be able to handle inadvertent entry into IMC with a better chance of survival. The flying may be somewhat ragged and unconfident but the survival of all on board will be far more likely than it will be with a pilot who has never undergone the training for an IMC Rating. The IMC rated pilot will need to climb at once to above Minimum Safety Altitude (MSA), call Air Traffic or Distress and Diversion, explain the predicament and, if appropriate, the limited degree of instrument flying capacity. This is likely to be a safer strategy than trying to fly out of cloud again when below MSA. Remember that low cloud often forms first around hills.

The options to fly 'VFR on top' and to fly Special VFR in controlled airspace in UK airspace can sometimes be useful privileges for the holder of a current IMC Rating and the training in radio navigation will always be useful.

Revalidation of Your Licence

Revalidation of Your Licence

The NPPL

You will need to renew your medical declaration at whatever interval is specified on the current declaration.

Renewal is either by way of a continuous experience process or by means of a Skill Test. The alternatives are

> EITHER

Have completed 6 hours flight time in the 12 month period preceding the flight including not less than 4 hours as pilot in command and have completed an instructional flight of at least 1 hour in the preceding 24 months:

> OR

Have undertaken and passed a Skill Test with an Authorised Examiner within the previous 12 months. The Examiner conducting the test will sign the Certificate of Revalidation Page of the NPPL and enter the date of the test but no expiry date will be shown in view of the fact that validation may, in the future be maintained via the experience route.

This information is correct at September 2004, but liable to future change. Up to date information can be found at www.nppl.uk.com/

The JAR PPL

Revalidation of the JAR-FCL licence is required every two years and this is accomplished by one of two alternatives.

1. You can undergo a proficiency check within the three months before the expiry of the licence.
2. Providing that within the twelve months before expiry you have flown 12 hours, including at least 6 as Pilot In Command, and made 12 take offs and 12 landings, you can undergo a training flight (as opposed to the proficiency check alternative) of at least an hour with an instructor.

To be effective your licence will need to be accompanied by an appropriate type or class rating and also a current medical. Other ratings, for example Multi or Instrument Ratings, all have their own revalidation requirements and these apply regardless of whether your licence is the old UK licence from the CAA or the new JAR-FCL type.

A single pilot single engine class rating is valid for two years, while a single pilot multi engine class rating is valid for only one year. To fly aircraft other than simple types, e.g. retractables, aircraft with variable pitch propellers, turbo engines or cabin pressurisation, you will need 'differences training'. This has to be certified in your logbook by the instructor.

To carry passengers you will need to have carried out three take offs and three landings within the previous 90 days. To carry passengers at night, in addition to a Night Rating or Night Qualification, you will need to have made at least one of your three take-offs and landings in the previous 90 days at night.

The requirements for the renewal of the required Class 2 medical are as follows:

Age	Validity
Under 30	5 years
39-49	2 years
50+	1 year

If you fly a Popular Flying Association aircraft type under a PFA supervised Permit to Fly you may consider it inappropriate to have to fly your biennial training flight with an instructor in a typical flying school aircraft. The two sorts of aircraft may have very different flying characteristics, which could make your training flight scarcely relevant to your normal operations. Furthermore, you may find the cost of hiring a flying school aircraft for an hour to be very expensive compared with the marginal cost of operating your own aircraft. The PFA operates an excellent coaching scheme which is designed to help pilots improve their skills and a flight with a coach counts as an 'instructional flight' for revalidation purposes. Many of the PFA coaches are also qualified to conduct a Skill Test.

Ditching

Ditching

As aircraft captain it is incumbent upon you before flying over water to ensure that you and your passengers are all wearing life jackets, and that you have on board, if possible, an Emergency Locator Beacon and a dinghy, both in readily accessible positions. In addition you should brief your passengers on the proper use of all the equipment and the correct ditching procedure.

Emergency locator beacons and/or Personal locator beacons have undergone a step change in recent years. The conventional beacon transmits on 121.5 Mhz and false alarms have become so numerous that they are often ignored unless the authorities have some particular reason to follow up an alarm signal. A Mayday call would be such a reason. The range of one of these beacons is line of sight and from a user in the water, that is going to be quite limited, so an accurate position report as part of the Mayday call is very important.

The more recent beacon transmits on 406 Mhz via satellites so that its range is world wide and, while these beacons continue to be relatively rare, false alarms will be equally rare. Better versions also transmit a GPS derived position and they signal as well on 121.5 Mhz so as to better enable precise location by a rescue helicopter. The 406 Mhz devices depend on suitable positioning of the appropriate satellite and this is assured only every 90 minutes, so that a prior Mayday call is essential for the pilot about to ditch in UK waters to avoid hypothermia occurring before the alarm has been given automatically.

In the event of ditching, you will all find yourselves in an entirely strange and confusing environment where you have very little time in which to perform various complicated, difficult and unusual operations. If you do not get these right more or less first time, you will probably not survive. It is vital, therefore that everybody knows what to do and has a realistic idea of what to expect. Without doubt, you should have dinghy-drill experience yourself and the more of your passengers who have this also, the better.

I consider that it is good practice to appoint one of the passengers as Dinghy Captain, who should take charge of the inflation of the dinghy after ditching. After all, you may be incapacitated and there should be someone else who has some idea of what to do. Furthermore, giving a passenger this duty will most likely make them think seriously about the operation. To this end I carry on board my aircraft the following list of Dinghy Captain's Duties which I give the Dinghy Captain to read at the beginning of the flight, and I usually encourage the other passengers to read it as well. It has been suggested that this might lead to alarm and despondency among my passengers but I have never detected this in practice. My view is that it is the unknown that we all fear the most, and information is a great defence against such fear.

The example below deals with a conventional four-seat low-wing aircraft with an accessible baggage compartment behind the rear seats and one door – a PA28, in fact. Different aircraft types will call for different instructions and you will need to draw up your own. You will find that the very act of doing this will make you think more deeply and constructively about the whole matter.

Dinghy Captain's Duties

Before take-off

Ensure that the dinghy is on the back seat if two or three up, or on top of the baggage area if four up. Either way, it must be secured before take-off with the seat harness or baggage straps. Ensure that you or whoever is going to have access to it knows how to release it and move it to the ditching position.

Ensure that the Emergency Locator Beacon (ELT) is put in somebody's charge. The ELT holder should have the unit to hand, and should know that to operate it the pin is pulled out and the unit kept roughly vertical with the aerial pointing upwards out of the water. All occupants should be wearing their lifejackets, uninflated, and should know both methods of inflating them. The double fastening bow should be in front and not at the wearer's side, so as to reduce the possibility of it catching on something.

Before ditching

Move the dinghy to its ditching position on the lap of the front passenger. The front passenger should open the door before ditching (both latches) and wedge something like a shoe in it so as to hold it ajar. The ELT holder should hang the unit around their neck on the cord provided so as to reduce the chance of it being left behind. Everybody should remove headsets, false teeth, spectacles and shoes. They should adopt the brace position and use something soft like a coat to reduce the possibility of impact damage to the head. There may be a substantial deceleration on ditching and the windscreen may be knocked out, so the dinghy should be kept low and central so as to avoid it inadvertently being lost through either the windscreen or the door.

Evacuation

The aim is to get all the occupants out of the aircraft with the ELT and the dinghy. The aircraft is not likely to float for long and there is clearly a need to evacuate promptly. On the other hand, a mad scramble to get out will most likely take longer than an orderly and thoughtful departure. Remember: undo your seat belt first and if in the back, know exactly how to tip forward the front passenger's seat-back. The order of evacuation is: front right-hand seat, taking dinghy and tying it on to self; rear right-hand; rear left-hand; front left-hand, who should check that the ELT is out.

Do not inflate your lifejacket until you are out of the aircraft or you may get stuck.

The aircraft may start sinking immediately after ditching. The outside water pressure may make it impossible at first to open the door. In this case it is necessary to wait for the water level to rise inside until the pressures have equalised.

You may find yourself having to get out of a submerged aircraft and it is easy to become disorientated and confused in such circumstances. Make sure that your seat belt is unfastened and nothing else is restraining your departure. Hold on to some identified part of the interior and work out which way to go in relation to that.

The rear side windows can be kicked out.

Getting into the dinghy

The aim is to get everybody into the dinghy as soon as possible. Again the approach should be thought-out and deliberate.

Inflate lifejackets. Inflate the dinghy by a very sharp pull on the cord, which must first be secured to someone or the dinghy might blow away.

Get the dinghy upright with the water pockets underneath full. The fittest person should get in first, using the webbing foothold loop. They can then counterbalance succeeding boarders and help them in. Exhaustion is the enemy here and it is much better to make a careful attempt at boarding – being sure of using the foothold effectively, and making one strong thrust upwards – than a series of hurried ineffective attempts which will quickly leave you unable to help yourself.

Where someone needs to be helped into the dinghy, first push them down into the water and then use the reaction as the water lifts them up again to assist your heave into the dinghy.

If you cannot get into the dinghy you should all stick together close to it and make sure that the ELT is properly deployed. Adopt a foetal position so as to limit heat loss. Face downwind of spray unless you have a spray hood on your lifejacket and are using it.

In the dinghy

Find the seasickness pills and make sure that everybody takes some immediately. Occupants of dinghies are very prone to seasickness, and vomiting loses valuable moisture and heat. Make sure that the ELT is properly deployed. Stream the sea anchor to give more stability and to reduce drift.

Bail and sponge-out the dinghy and wring out clothing where possible. Close the canopy. Check out the supply of flares and other equipment.

Remember

You will survive in the sea for about one or two hours in British waters, which should be ample time for a helicopter rescue providing that it can find you. The ELT is very important here.

You can survive for days in the dinghy.

Around Britain you will become too cold and exhausted to help yourself after about ten minutes in the water, so it is important to get into the dinghy without delay and without unnecessary expenditure of effort.

Organisations and Useful Addresses

Organisations and Useful Addresses

Aeronautical Information Service
NATS, AIS Central Office
First Floor, Control Tower Building
Heathrow Airport
Hounslow
Middx TW6 1JJ
Tel: 020 8745 3456
Fax: 020 8745 3453
www.ais.org.uk
For air traffic and navigational information throughout the world.

Air Accident Investigation Branch
Berkshire Copse Road
Aldershot
Hants GU11 2HH
Tel: 01252 510300
www.dft.gov.uk/ (via 'Accidents')
All UK accidents involving injury or damage must be reported promptly to AAIB. The website has all past accident reports.

The Air League
4 Hamilton Place
London W1V 0BQ
Tel: 020 7491 0470
Fax: 020 7499 7261
www.airleague.co.uk
A body dedicated to popularising aviation in all forms.

The Aircraft Owner & Pilots Association
50a Cambridge Street
London SW1V 4BR
Tel: 020 7834 5631
Fax: 020 7834 8623
www.aopa.co.uk
AOPA represents everyone involved in General Aviation and every private pilot ought to join so as to support this vital body.

Air Training Corps
Headquarters Air Cadets
RAF College
Cranwell
Sleaford
Lincs
NG34 8HB
Tel: 01400 261201 ext 7630
or try local telephone directory
www.aircadet.net
Offers training and some flying experience for boys and girls between 13 and 18.a

British Aerobatic Association
White Waltham Airfield
Maidenhead
Berks SL6 3NJ
Tel: 01455 617211
www.aerobatics.org.uk

British Microlight Aircraft Association
The Bullring
Deddington
Oxfordshire
OX15 0TT
Tel 01869 338888
www.bmaa.org

British Women Pilots Association
Rochester Airport
Chatham
Kent ME5 9SD
Tel: 01614 816340
www.bwpa.demon.co.uk

Civil Aviation Authority
Flight Crew Licensing
Aviation House
Gatwick Airport South
West Sussex RH6 0YR
Tel: 01293 573700
Fax: 01293 573996
www.caa.co.uk
For all inquiries about UK and JAA/EASA licences and ratings

General Aviation Safety Council
Rochester Airport
Chatham
Kent
ME5 9SD
Tel 01634 200203
www.gasco.org.uk
A body supported by most of the UK General Aviation organisations, including the CAA. It is devoted to improving GA's safety record and publishes 'Flight Safety' every quarter.

Guild of Air Pilots & Air Navigators
Cobham House
291 Gray's Inn Road
London WC1X 8QF
Tel: 020 7837 3323
www.hiway.co.uk/gapan
A senior body of pilots and navigators.

Met Office
Fitzroy Road
Exeter
Devon EX1 3PB
Tel 01392 886513
www.metoffice.com.

Popular Flying Association
Turweston Aerodrome
Brackley
Northants
Tel: 01280 846 786
Fax: 01280 846 780
www.pfa.org.uk
Represents pilots and home builders of aircraft interested in simple and inexpensive aviation. Runs a network of local groups, Europe's biggest annual rally of private aircraft and a monthly magazine.

PPL/IR Europe
c/o Ole Henriksen
Le Clos au Comte
Castel
Guernsey, CI
Tel: 01481 52665
Fax: 01481 52563
www.pplir.org
A European network of private pilots interested in instrument flying. Publishes a two monthly journal

Royal Aero Club
Kimberley House
Vaughan Way
Leicester LE1 4SG
Tel: 0116 253 1051
Fax: 0116 251 5939
www.royalaeroclub.org
The senior aeronautical body mostly concerned with air racing and record attempts

Pilot Supplies, Aircraft and Glider Accessories:

Airplan Flight Equipment Ltd
Manchester Pilot Shop
1a Ringway Trading Estate
Shadowmoss Road
Manchester M22 5LH
Tel: 0161 499 0023
Fax: 0161 499 0298
e-mail: enquiries@afeonline.com
www.afeonline.com

Oxford Airport Pilot Shop
Oxford Airport
Kiddlington
Oxford
OX5 1QX
Tel: 01865 841441
Fax: 01865 842495
e-mail: tech@afeonline.com
www.afeonline.com

Index

Index